Silent Alarm

Silent Alarm

On the Edge with a Deaf EMT

Steven L. Schrader

Gallaudet University Press • Washington, D.C.

The characters and events in this story are entirely true. If anyone should dispute this, the author will be flattered.

Gallaudet University Press
Washington, DC 20002

Library of Congress Cataloging-in-Publication Data

Schrader, Steven L., 1957–
    Silent alarm : on the edge with a deaf EMT / Steven L. Schrader.
        p.   cm.
        ISBN 1–56368–044–0 (alk. paper)
        1. Schrader, Steven L., 1957– . 2. Deaf emergency medical
technicians—Georgia—Geography. 3. Emergency medical services—
Georgia—Anecdotes. I. Title.
    RA645.6.G4S37   1995
    610.69'53—dc20   95–34074
                                             CIP

Book design by Dennis Anderson
Jacket photograph by L. Lause/Superstock

*To the Eastern North Carolina School for the Deaf,
and in loving memory of Pop Conn, my war hero,
and Jimmy Massey*

To my precious wife, Nancy Carol Patrick, I love you.

Contents

Acknowledgments

*T*his being an autobiography, I have my mother, my wife, a few APD officers, Chief Henry Phillips, and brother firefighters the late Sgt. Gus Swaney and Jimmy Massey to thank. I never could have done it without their support, encouragement, and guidance.

And there is a special place in my heart for Ivey Pittle Wallace and Elaine Costello of Gallaudet University Press. Their concern and support for me during my illness was my source of motivation as well as a blessing.

Silent Alarm

Introduction

One rainy night, almost seven years after I resigned from Grady Emergency Medical Services in downtown Atlanta, Georgia, I ran into Cookie and her husband at Hartsfield International Airport. I was on my way to Washington, D.C., to hand in the final draft of this book when we met by chance. She hadn't aged a bit and was still as warm-hearted and compassionate as I remembered from the old days. It took her a moment or two to recognize me— her old partner from the evening watch. It was Cookie's first flight and she looked nervous as we boarded the last night flight out of Atlanta bound for Dulles Airport. As the lightning bolts flashed in the heavens below us and isolated mountain towns crawled slowly past, we became deeply engrossed in conversation about the old days. As she began to recount a war story, the inside of the airplane transformed itself into an ambulance, and I could visualize us on our way to a call.

She told me the old guys were still there, mostly on the day watch, and she said they still talked about "Catfish." That's me. Whenever I started to get "lost" in her story, Cookie would stop talking until I looked her in the face, and that would bring back another flashback. I recalled her curtly saying, "LOOK AT ME when I'm talking to you!" I remembered her best for being a mother to me, always looking after me and listening to my sick jokes. Cookie used to like a favorite joke of mine and she often repeated it to the others. "What do you call a deaf man who robs a 7-Eleven store?" She'd give them a moment to think before saying, "Deaf AND dumb!"

As the plane suddenly dipped to the left and then to the right before straightening itself on a new heading, Cookie sought reassurance from her quiet husband before continuing. "I never thought of you as a deaf EMT," she said. That was just what I needed to hear because I'd been wondering if it was difficult to work with a deaf EMT (emergency medical technician). She laughed and leaned over closer to my ear, "Every time I hear your nickname I remember how you could make me laugh through an entire shift and how protective you were of your female partners. You were very, very good at talking to people, calming them down when no one else could. You just knew how to talk to people. Don't you remember?" I was reminded of several suicide calls. "Oh, and your driving, too!" I laughed and shuddered at the same time.

Somehow, the bulkwall in front of us shimmered into a scene of a side street, on the south side of Atlanta and I was watching myself from a distance as I struggled to take out the stretcher from the back of an ambulance. I had no idea as to what that call was about. It was just one of thousands under my belt. After a while, the calls become routine and almost boring; they're all the same, all the damn time.

I told Cookie how hard it was to suddenly become a civilian after being an EMT for so damn long. It was pure cold turkey. Not a very good thing to do without some professional counseling.

I think about the streets sometimes and the war still raging into the nights. When an ambulance or a fire truck passes me by, with siren wailing mournfully and the lights flashing red and white, I still feel a deep pang of guilt. I think about all the corpses, false hopes and promises, living for the six-o-clock news, my suicide attempt, and living with the memory of dead partners and patients alike. There was also the booze and smoking pot with cops and robbers, endless good times and the same amount of bad times. Sheer damn boredom that could make a grown man cry would suddenly turn horrific. We expected the unexpected and when we were lucky, we helped those who really needed it.

The Ambulance Department of Grady Emergency Medical Services (EMS) based out of Grady Memorial Hospital in Atlanta, lived by the motto, "We cheat Death!" I can honestly proclaim that no patients "died" on me while in my or another Grady EMT's immediate care: not on the way to a hospital or at any other time that the patient might be in peril. The Grim Reaper, try as he might, could only wait until I signed the patient over to a nurse in the emergency room. After the trip report sheet had been signed, the patient could die, then. Someone else could take over C P and damn R!

To this day, I do not know how I survived the streets, Grady EMS, all the private ambulance services that plagued the city of Atlanta and the rest of Fulton County, and the rest of the obstacles I encountered along the way. I dealt with it all with my profound hearing loss and came out on top, at least I thought so. I did the best I could, but it took years off my life, mentally and physically.

Just then, the captain announced over the intercom, "Flight attendants, prepare for landing." The late-night flight from Atlanta began its final approach to Dulles. Heavy fog blanketed the runways. The ninety-minute flight appeared to have taken only fifteen minutes. Cookie and I parted with hugs, and I promised her that I would return to Grady Hospital to visit the guys and maybe ride out with them. It would be like old times.

1

The Early Years

I was born at Saint Francis Catholic Hospital in Beech Grove, Indiana, just outside of Indianapolis, on November 30, 1957. My mother had endured thirty-six hours of labor complicated by pneumonia. She was given last rites by the hospital priest after doctors determined she might not survive the delivery.

My father begged the hospital to save his wife and let the baby die, but they insisted on trying to save the baby, even if it cost my mother her life. She had contracted German measles during her pregnancy, and at that time there was no vaccine for the disease. Thousands of children were born deaf, blind, or both. During the last trimester, she developed pneumonia, and the prognosis remained uncertain. A week later, and without any surgical procedures, I was removed from the incubator and taken home with my mother. The doctors proclaimed me to be normal, and the nuns blessed us as a miracle. My profound hearing loss, a result of the German measles, was not discovered until three years later.

One of my earliest childhood memories is of living at Camp Pendleton, near San Diego, California, on a Marine Corps base. My father worked as chief of the communication center for the base, and my mother had a full-time job at a title insurance company. To earn extra money she did the laundry for my father's boss, Major Gregory "Pappy" Boyington. The major is known as the leader of the Black Sheep Squadron—a group of pilots who flew in the Pacific Theater during World War II. But he is remembered because of an old TV series. The portrayal of the ace flyer apparently was accurate, including its depiction of his excessive alcohol consumption. While Mother did Boyington's dirty laundry, my father tended to the war hero in the same way a mother does her child. Years later, Major Boyington was buried with full military honors in Arlington, Virginia, just below the marker for the seven astronauts who died in the Challenger explosion.

At the height of the Vietnam War, my father disappeared from my childhood to fight an undeclared war in Southeast Asia. He served as a helicopter machine-gunner and crew chief for more than three tours. Something happened over there, and when I saw him again, I knew my real father had died in the jungle and come home in the guise of a skeletal and disillusioned soldier. Only after I became a firefighter and an EMT did I begin to understand some of what he was trying to forget. He used to smile when he mentioned that he had been assigned to take care of Walter Cronkite, the CBS newscaster, when Cronkite was in Vietnam to do a special. And I would smile right back at him when I mentioned that Walter Cronkite rode with me and my partner for a TV special that dealt with violence in America. Most of the time, Walter just muttered under his breath, "Goddamn!"

When my father was still at Camp Pendleton, my mother took me to the base hospital for my annual physical. I was two years old. She told the navy physician that I was not speaking clearly and that I often did not respond to spoken commands. He could find nothing wrong with me. A short time later, after my sister was born, my father was transferred to Camp Lejeune in North Carolina, where again a doctor proclaimed me to be a healthy, normal little boy. In response to my mother's concern about my speech, the doctor replied, "Your child is not tongue-tied, and the only thing he is going to grow out of is his clothes." The doctor did, however, suspect I had a hearing loss, so he recommended that I go to a county clinic for further evaluation by a caseworker. The caseworker told my mother that I was severely retarded and should be institutionalized. My mother asked for a second opinion from another caseworker, who determined that I had a hearing and speech disability. With my mother's grateful approval, she began a program of therapy twice a week, as well as a series of tests to determine my mental health and intelligence.

After getting these results, the doctor sent my father and me to the University of North Carolina at Chapel Hill for an extensive hearing evaluation to determine the extent of my hearing loss and to find a suitable hearing aid for me to wear. At the end of an anxious week, we returned to Chapel Hill to learn that I had a severe hearing loss, and we picked up my new hearing aid–a box-style body aid with a double-Y cord for the ear molds. I thought it weighed a ton and a half. While we were at the university clinic, my parents learned about the new school for the deaf in Wilson. I still wonder how many deaf kids were placed in institutions based on the mistaken idea that they were retarded, and I still shudder at the thought.

During the 1950s the North Carolina School for the Deaf in Morganton had been in serious need of expansion, testimony to the ever-increasing number of deaf children born as the result of several epidemics that had plagued different parts of the country over a period of time. As it was, the school in Morganton was the fourth-largest residential education program of its kind in the United States. It had a long waiting list, which induced the state advisory budget committee to prepare a budget request for a second institution. A number of parents of deaf children, mainly from the eastern part of the state, urged members of the North Carolina Assembly to consider the establishment of another school similar to the one at Morganton.

In the fall of 1960 the state legislature approved the development of a new school at a cost of $2.5 million. Wilson was decided on as the new site after the Eastern North Carolina Sanitarium, with two well-constructed brick buildings, was made available to the state without cost. On April 25, 1964, eighty-eight students, aged five through ten, began their education at the Eastern North Carolina School for the Deaf. Seventy-two of the students were transfers from the school in Morganton, while the other sixteen children were being enrolled in school for the first time.

In the late summer of 1964, at the age of six, I began my education at the Eastern North Carolina School for the Deaf (ENCSD) in Wilson. It still seems like only yesterday. The hot air, perfumed with the aroma of golden tobacco leaves, mixed with the exhaust fumes from the smoke-belching rigs hauling the harvest toward the warehouses in town. Old Highway 301 stretched as far as the eye could see then. You could see from the end of the northern horizon to the end of the southern horizon, with the tobacco fields in between dotted with hundreds of black and migrant workers. The view from the window of our dormitory revealed tobacco fields that dominated the countryside with barely a patch or two of forest to break up the rich landscape.

Alongside the southbound lane of 301 stood a five-foot-high chain-link fence separating the highway from the Eastern North Carolina School for the Deaf. Most sunny afternoons, after class was let out, kids would line up alongside the inside fence to wave frantically at each passing truck. They could feel the shock of the hot wind blowing against their faces, though their ears could barely hear the blowing horns. It became a daily ritual—we waved excitedly and truck drivers passing by responded with a cacophony of horn blowing, which delighted the deaf children. One day a little boy suddenly turned to his houseparent and excitedly signed, "Me hear! Me hear!" It brought a smile to his face.

The Eastern North Carolina School for the Deaf is a non-sectarian deaf educational institution. Hearing-impaired students could attend if it was determined that they were unable to profit from a regular public school and were of sound mind. Those who were classified as feeble-minded or handicapped were not eligible and were referred elsewhere. The tuition was free for students who resided in the state of North Carolina. The primary function of the school was to give deaf children a means of communication so that they could acquire an education and learn a trade. The second function involved teaching the students the importance of self-reliance, so that they could become intelligent and confident human beings, capable of taking their rightful place in society.

The students were placed in one of three basic classifications, designed to ensure that each child was placed in an appropriate class. From my perspective these "appropriate" classes consisted of three categories: hopeless, dumb, and smart. The last group was composed of students whose hearing ability was sufficient to allow them to acquire language through a hearing aid and lipreading. Ironically, I was placed in this category not by the "experts," but by the students. The school initially categorized my hearing loss as "hopeless," even though I had some residual hearing.

Our first years of instruction focused on speech, lipreading, and communication. We learned English through sounds, gradually building words and sentences from isolated syllables. This was the beginning of a new era, moving beyond teaching the deaf by writing pad and pencil, to teaching with total communication, that is, both sign language and oral language. The students were grouped in classes averaging from eight to ten each.

Recreation was my favorite part of growing up at the school. There were plenty of activities, including Boy Scouts and field trips, and a well-balanced athletic program. There will never be another football team like the one I was on. Everyone was much bigger than I was, and most of us were stupid enough not to know what pain was. Our record remains unsurpassed, with ten wins and no losses—the other teams never even scored against us, and most of our scores were up in the forties. I think some of the other teams were paralyzed with fear at the thought of facing what they perceived to be deaf and dumb football players who could only grunt and growl. I can vouch for the fact that the coach was a man to fear if he was pissed off. He was a big man of Indian blood, with the profile of a great warrior. His signing was smooth, graceful, and slow. When he said good morning, it looked like an eagle rising majestically in the sky of the morning sun.

Manners, morals, and character building played a bigger part in our lives than we realized at the time. Our houseparent was another big guy who could instill fear in our hearts if we even thought about some kind of misdeed. He was a big influence on me, and he helped prepare me for the "real" world. His pet peeve was my constant talking without signing to other hearing-impaired friends.

It took nearly half a lifetime to realize that the education I received from ENCSD was far superior to that available in the regular public school system. After completing the eighth grade at ENCSD, which did not offer courses beyond that level, most students transferred to the high school department at the North Carolina School for the Deaf (NCSD) at Morganton, in the foothills of the mountains. After six months there I dropped out to enroll as a sophomore at Walter Page Senior High School in Greensboro, North Carolina. If I had known then what I know now, I would have stayed at NCSD, instead of mainstreaming into a public high school. It was the first mistake of my life, although it turned out to be a blessing in disguise. During this time in my life, my sister Sissy was a vital link between me and the outside world. I relied on her contacts and her advice, even about how I should dress, as I tried to adjust to the "real" world of a public high school.

The processing of new students into Walter Page High involved a meeting with an advisor and counselor, much like colleges have for new freshmen. At first the counselor was concerned about my disability and suggested that I enroll in the school's special education class for slower students or the severely handicapped. I told him right away that I would be fine in a regular class. My only complaint was the lack of education that was available even in the regular program. There were forty to fifty kids for each teacher. In fact, I don't recall having to do homework during the year I was there. My grades dropped to low C's and D's, as opposed

to the A's and B's I had earned at ENCSD. Even my place-
ment near the teacher, on the front row, didn't help much
because of all the talking and carrying on from the rest of
the class. The teacher seemed to spend a lot of time escort-
ing students from the classroom to detention hall.

Part of the problem was that I was more concerned with
making new friends than I was with going to school and
learning. It was important to me to find out whether I could
hang out with the guys in the bathroom and maybe share
a butt with them. When I had been at ENCSD, those of
us who were hard of hearing tried to be more like the hearing students with new stereos and long hair. We started to
hang out by ourselves and talk verbally. It seemed so much
easier just to talk rather than to use fingers and hands to
communicate. We wouldn't use sign language when talking to each other, much to the disgust of the other deaf
students.

After I enrolled at Walter Page High in Greensboro, my
life became a series of challenges, the first of which was my
participation in the Navy Junior Reserve Officers Training
Corps (ROTC), as a seaman cadet in the Third Squadron.
I was eventually promoted to third-class petty officer with
a dual spot as a member of both the rifle team and the color
guard. As part of this new challenge, of course, the long
hair had to come off and the proper attire worn for the initial interview. I believe that being a member of an (almost)
all-black rifle drill team was one of the most incredible things
I have ever done. I had to call on all of my senses, including those I didn't know I had, using both hearing aids with
extra batteries in every pocket and a fierce determination
to succeed at something, anything. I listened carefully and
said little, and tried not to make the same mistake twice.

I could perform precise military rifle and drilling maneuvers with the best of them during football games and ceremonies, just so long as the commander did not change the format at the last minute. I had to memorize each step and procedure and keep my timing perfect without deviating by a second. My position in the ranks was next to the commander, so that I could be sure to hear the commands. It took hours to perfect the moves. I can still hear the jeering and teasing from the predominantly black crowd in the benches, and I can't say that I blamed them. A white man in a sea of black uniformed students did look rather odd.

One of my fondest memories of that time was of a summer trip to Charleston, South Carolina, in 1975, to the naval base on the harbor. It was time for the annual training exercises based on what we had learned all year long in the classroom. We were assigned to the Anti-Mine Warfare School while barracked near the docks containing naval patrol vessels equipped for anti-mining operations. These particular boats had just returned from Vietnam the year before. I had been assigned to work a shift as a fire watch officer, or FWO, to keep watch on our floor for signs of smoke or fire while the others slept. As I looked out the large porthole of the barracks, I could see Fort Sumter in the middle of the Charleston harbor. I remember thinking then that being an FWO was the closest I was ever going to come to being a firefighter, which had been a tradition in my family dating back to the Civil War and my great-great-grandfather, Alexander Von Schroeder. My father's last name at birth had been spelled *Schroeder,* as was that of one of his brothers. The other three brothers had it spelled *Schrader* on their birth certificates. I have relatives in Michigan with the last name spelled as *Shrader,* leaving the *c* out.

Alexander had come straight from the Prussian War as an officer in a cavalry unit to enlist in the United States

Army under Ulysses S. Grant. With a bounty of $300 and a commission as a lieutenant colonel, he was assigned as an aide-de-camp in the Fourteenth Army Corps. He served with distinction during the Civil War, and participated in the March through Georgia with William Sherman's army before being mustered out in early 1865. He chose to remain in the country and start a family in the Mississippi River town of Paducah, Kentucky. He became the town's first fire chief, the first of a long line of Schraders and Schroeders to work in that profession. I was determined not to break the tradition just because I wore bilateral hearing aids.

As I watched a light frigate kick its fantail for a new heading out toward the ocean, I remembered the first time that I experienced the desire to become a firefighter. I was in the fifth grade at ENCSD, when we noted a dark cloud spilling into the Carolina blue sky during social science class. The teacher was discussing the geography of Europe when she noticed a tremendous amount of smoke billowing into the trees before reaching the sky. The whole class yelped in glee as we stormed for the windows and watched in awe the most incredible show on earth. Just a week before, the Wilson Fire Department had been to our school to present its Fire Prevention Program. Now we were seeing them in action.

Across the football field and the deep creek beyond was a trailer park whose residents were mostly migrant workers and tobacco pickers. One of the trailers had caught fire at one end and was lit up like a giant cigar. The angry fingers of flame rapidly consumed the thin melting walls while spitting out unburned combustible materials amidst the black smoke. A Seagrave fire engine, with red lights flashing and its siren dying after wailing through town, pulled up to the nearest hydrant and unloaded a three-inch supply line. A few seconds later another truck pulled past the first to stop in front of the burning trailer. Several firefighters spilled out of the cab while two more jumped off the tailboard. Another man pulled off several sections of the fire hose.

As if in a dream, I watched in amazement as a firefighter approached the front door of the trailer with his helmet turned backward. He used the long neck of the helmet as a shield against the heat. With every twist and turn of the wind, the smoke would swallow the man whole and then release him. Flame danced through the sooty smoke while the man took the proffered nozzle and disappeared through the gate of hell as if it were just another stroll through the fire-training tower at the local fire academy.

Meanwhile, the little trailer park had turned into a parking lot choked with fire trucks and police vehicles. Some of the trucks interconnected tandem-style with each other as sections of hose were laid out in a woven pattern. Water surged back and forth in a confluence of streams. Water forced its way through the melting walls while the lone firefighter fought a losing battle from the inside. I was amazed at how effortlessly the firefighters coordinated their activities. I believe that firefighting was in my blood before I had even heard about the family tradition. The only question was, how could I become a firefighter?

2

In Pursuit of a Dream

I had at one point seriously considered enlisting in the navy after graduation from high school, but I learned that all of my deaf friends from the Eastern North Carolina School for the Deaf were planning to attend Gallaudet College in Washington, D.C., starting in the fall of 1976. There was something magic about the name *Gallaudet* that made me want to go, too. I had heard about it all my life, and looked forward to going to college there someday.

I withdrew from Walter Page Senior High School and attended Guilford Technical Institution in Jamestown, just south of Greensboro. I planned to take the General Equivalency Diploma (GED) test and apply for college the day after I received my test results.

Two months later, I found myself on the campus of Gallaudet College, with the Capitol and the Washington Monument as backdrop. I was at a party for the students from North Carolina when I received notification from a priest that my sister Sissy had been seriously injured in an automobile accident. It was a Monday night, and the end of my first day of college. Needless to say, I was devastated.

Sissy had just turned sixteen and had been excited to learn that I would not be needing the car, a yellow Toyota Corolla, while I was away at college. Life was just beginning to look good for her again. She had gotten a job at Hardee's and was anxious to start school again after having dropped out the year before. Apparently Sissy and two of her best friends, Tracey and Vada, were under the influence of alcohol and driving to a party at a friend's house. Sissy lost control of the car when the right front tire dropped off the shoulder on a sharp curve. She jerked the car back toward the road, causing it to bound sideways and slam head on into another car coming from the opposite direction. Tracey was ejected through the front window and died of massive head injuries. Vada and Sissy were transported to different hospitals and placed in their intensive care units. The other driver miraculously suffered no injuries.

I flew home on a Piedmont Airlines prop plane and hurried to Moses Cone Memorial Hospital to be at my sister's side. She died five days later, after two full arrests. She had never really had any chance of surviving the injury to her spinal cord, and the base of her brain had all but snapped in half. The only visible trauma was to her right ear, which had been reattached surgically and was covered with a large bulk trauma dressing.

All I could think about was how much Sissy loved me and how very proud of me she had been, for being deaf of all things. My mother once asked me, "Did you know that Sissy wanted to be deaf, too?" We buried her at Westminster Memorial Garden in Greensboro, North Carolina, head to foot with Tracy. Vada recovered after months of therapy and treatment. For the next two years, Vada refused to see me. I wondered if it had anything to do with the lawsuits against my family from all of the parties involved.

Mom and Pop began a series of reluctant separations, often on different sides of the country, while I tried to get my life in order. Eventually my dad obtained a better position as a communications specialist with the Hammermill Paper Company in Erie, Pennsylvania. Mom moved out of her YWCA apartment in Raleigh, North Carolina, and met Pop in Erie in time for the first snow-flake to fall. I prepared to resign from Moses Cone Memorial Hospital, where I had been working as an orderly and morgue assistant. My parents' bankruptcy proceedings prohibited me from returning to Gallaudet. I had to go to work and start supporting myself.

For some reason, after Sissy's death I felt compelled to work for the same hospital where she had died. I remembered the machines and all the accessories surrounding my sister. The wires and tubes with blood, fluid, and medication kept close human contact to a minimum. I felt completely helpless to do anything for her. I guess that working as an orderly was my way of helping others through her spirit, in a roundabout way.

At this same time the hospital had received grant money to initiate a training program for orderlies and nursing assistants, who would be placed in jobs at the hospital after completion of the program. I was accepted into the program, and began work.

Upon completion of the required eighty hours' training, I was posted in the ICU and assigned to work with the same nurse who had had ultimate responsibility for the care of Sissy. It came as quite a shock to her when I was introduced to her by the head nurse. It hadn't been more than sixty days since Sissy died. Sadly, this same nurse became my patient three weeks later when she was brought in from the emergency room, in a coma from an automobile accident. Her Volkswagen had hydroplaned and smashed into a bridge span. When I had to leave for Erie, she was still in a coma, and I never heard what happened to her.

I will always remember the little girl who had cystic fibrosis, a chronic lung disease. She was forced to either sit up or risk death by lying down. She was barely able to breathe sitting up, and I could see the fear in her tired eyes. She knew that if she lay her head down to sleep, she would die. She was only nine years old and as pretty a little girl as I've ever seen. Her name was Ashley, and she asked me to be her friend, to hold her hand, to remind her to breathe and stay awake, and to prop her up with all kinds of pillows so she could take catnaps. It got so I couldn't leave her alone, and the nurses in ICU took up the slack for me while I stayed by her side for two weeks. I asked her once, "What do you want to do when you get out of school?" She would simply whisper a reply, "I want to be a nurse."

On her last day on earth, I asked her if I could go home and get cleaned up and bring more flowers and games for her to play with. She smiled and said yes. I kissed her on the forehead and told her I would be right back. When I returned to the hospital and walked into the ICU, I saw Ashley's bed empty and the sheets replaced. One of the nurses came out of the station and tried to explain, but I turned and ran out into the hallway for the elevators. On the way down, I was fumbling with a large set of keys, looking for the key to the morgue. After what seemed like forever, I reached the end of the hallway, threw open the door, and went straight to the first drawer. I opened each drawer and couldn't find Ashley in any one of them. I looked at the clipboard on the desk and scanned the list for her name. She had already been taken away to a funeral home.

They told me after I left that Ashley waited until nobody was watching her. She pushed the pillows away and lay down on the bed with her head on the pillow for the first time in a long time. She took her last breath and died quietly after a minute or two. I prayed that Sissy would be at the gate of heaven, waiting for my little friend.

My contact with deaf people became a thing of the past when I left North Carolina after resigning from my job as an orderly at Moses Cone Memorial Hospital. In the winter of 1977, I said goodbye to close friends from my old school and departed reluctantly for Erie, Pennsylvania, sandwiched between New York and Ohio, to meet my parents. They had reconciled after a trial separation, and I was just beginning to experience the feeling of having no idea what I wanted to do next. Everything had changed the minute Sissy died. My desire to study prelaw at Gallaudet and eventually become a lawyer had been shattered like a broken mirror. This had been my mother's dream for me, as she had never had the opportunity to go to college, and had worked with a law firm as a legal assistant.

Erie is basically an industrial town. It reeked of the products made by the biggest employer there, Hammermill Paper, where my father was employed as a communications specialist. Lake Erie resembled an ocean in some ways. The water was always soft and flat, with an occasional water spout to stir the seaweed. The seaweed had turned the lake green and choked most of the beaches with a fresh carpet of the stuff, but further back from the breaking waves the beaches were a harsh white in the Yankee sun. Sunsets were always me and my girl's favorite time to sit on a dock of the bay created by the long peninsula that jutted out like an arm from the mainland. We could hold hands and watch the oil tankers pass slowly by on the far horizon as the sun sank behind the low-lying bank of clouds turned blood-red and orange. When the stars appeared and the moon cast its beams across the water, we'd go home to my new apartment, listen to Lynard Skynard, drink Rolling Rock, and wait for my life to begin.

I spent the rest of the summer being the laziest boy in America. I spent hour upon hour at the old gravel pit underneath a wooden covered bridge. A sparkling cold spring fed the pit with a long rope attached to a giant elm tree, inviting anyone to swing out and jump into the crystal blue water. The gravel pit, a by-product of the days when rocks were used for building materials and cement, was rumored to be bottomless. We used the covered bridge either as a diving platform or as a place to lie on warm wooden beams and let the sun lure us into slumber. The aroma of marijuana scented our little world while clouds of the exhaled smoke rose slowly through the canopy of the forest.

The atmosphere signaled to me the end of an era that had been long in dying, since all the older hippies had become businesspeople and the like. Flower power, free love, and peace soon faded along with long hair and bell-bottom jeans. The Vietnam War was still fresh in our minds, and the country was still recovering from the economic and social impact of it all. The sexual revolution was in full swing and the miniskirt got longer, while President Nixon was still enjoying some measure of popularity.

I knew it was time to move on, but my mother beat me to it. She handed me a phone book and turned to the hospital section. "Why don't you work for one of these hospitals? Maybe they can help you get back into school." She was right, of course. I didn't have to go looking for a job as a printer, a trade I had learned at the Morganton School for the Deaf. I hated that trade. I had envied some of my older deaf friends who were working for high-paying corporations and making good money. I had already gotten my training as an orderly at Moses Cone Hospital and saw no reason why I couldn't keep it up. I saw a door opening at the far end of a tunnel, and ideas started to become solid plans. I realized that to be a firefighter, I had to get through the medical aspect of the training and use it as a stepping-stone to the fire department itself.

It was at Moses Cone that I first encountered a North Carolina emergency medical technician, and I fell in love with the patch. I had never heard of that job classification and did not quite understand the job description other than the fact that the patch signified a person who did emergency work. When the man stepped off the elevator, I decided then that I wanted to do something like that, but I had no idea how to go about it. I just knew I wanted to do more than push hospital gurneys all over the floors and clean dead bodies in the morgue for the rest of my life. I knew there was a fire waiting to be put out, someday.

I took a page out of the phone book and went knocking on personnel office doors and asking for work as an orderly. The first hospital I went to, Doctors Osteopathic Hospital near downtown Erie, hired me to work on the surgical floor. They never even asked me if I had a disability. They couldn't tell I wore hearing aids under my long hair. One nurse I worked with finally asked me if I had a cleft palate inside my mouth since she couldn't see any obvious scarring on my lips. I told her no, but that I was deaf. She laughed and walked away, saying, "Yeah, right!" I was amazed. I decided that if I could work on my speech impediment that I could get away with being deaf, and maybe even work my way into the fire department. I had always feared discrimination, especially in the medical field. People always reminded me that I had a speech impediment, and children were always asking what I was wearing in my ear. Strangely enough, I decided to use the cleft-palate story to account for my speech impediment and to try to rely on my skills as a lipreader. At that time, neither I, nor any other deaf person for that matter, knew that there would ever be an Americans with Disabilities Act to protect us from discrimination. I often placed myself in a hearing person's shoes and asked myself if I would hire a deaf man to be responsible for people's lives if I weren't familiar with deaf culture.

As always during the first week of October, it snowed and snowed until I got sick of it. Erie continued to function as if this were nothing out of the ordinary. The northern wind would come roaring over the water with such force that waves froze in midbreak to form a natural barrier of crazy patterns of salty icicles. Beyond the barrier you could count dozens of small fishing shacks spread out over the frozen lake with their four-wheel drive trucks and a few station wagons parked nearby. A friend of mine took me out over the frozen water and beyond the structures to within a mile of a river cut through the lake by U.S. Coast Guard ice-breakers, which allowed oil tankers to sail to their destinations. Even though the ice was several feet thick and rock solid, I could feel a miniature earthquake every time an oil tanker passed by. I still remember that experience as a mixture of fear and amazement. The sun fought a losing battle against the cold, and life went on in Erie. A friend of mine told me that I could walk clear across the water and reach Canada if it weren't for the rivers cut in by the Coast Guard. Instead, I headed back to North Carolina and married an old sweetheart from the Eastern North Carolina School for the Deaf in Wilson. Gina had been the quietest girl I knew at school, smiling and always sweet to everyone.

Gina and I married in a country church just outside of Raleigh, North Carolina, in the presence of a couple of friends and my mother. Once again, my parents were forced to separate while my father headed to Chicago to begin work as a communication specialist for Flying Tiger, a cargo airline based at O'Hare Airport. Mother went back to a different title insurance company in Raleigh and moved back into the YWCA while Gina and I tried to get on our feet. I went to work as an orderly for a local hospital and Gina became pregnant with our first child. She stayed home and took care of the house. My paycheck was just not enough for us to live on, so we moved to Indianapolis to live with my grandparents while I worked as an emergency room attendant at the hospital where I was born. I was still basically working as an orderly—the title had changed but the job was the same. I did all the dirty jobs that the nurses, doctors, and janitors didn't have time for. Still, no one knew I was deaf. I was getting good at this. Meanwhile, my father couldn't stand the Chicago winter and moved to Los Angeles, and shortly thereafter sent for my mother.

After a couple of paychecks, Gina and I moved into our own "apartment." It was a room at the Wisconsin Hotel in downtown Indianapolis and was considered a third-rate flea-bag hotel. Each floor shared a bathroom at the end of the hallway. If you wanted to watch television, you had to walk down eighteen floors to the lobby and watch it there. The elevator was constantly out of service. There were no air conditioners, and we tried to breathe the humid and rancid air of downtown that came through the large window. I barely made enough to pay our rent and make our car payment. The pay at the hospital didn't improve until I had completed a six-month probationary period. Until then we lived on peanut butter and jelly and baloney sandwiches. To pay for baloney and bread, I would give a pint of plasma at a local clinic, for which I was paid five dollars. Meanwhile, we had learned that Gina was expecting our first child.

After a few more paychecks, we finally found a nice apartment a few blocks over from the Wisconsin Hotel. We moved in with only two camp cots to sleep on. Whenever I think about that apartment, I am reminded of the night we went to bed and something came to visit me. Somehow, I woke to see our large bay window open halfway as a long wisp of white smoke entered the apartment. Just as I started to get up and investigate, five icy fingers grabbed my head and turned me toward the wall away from the window. It scared the living shit out of me. I couldn't scream or move a muscle for as long as I felt those fingers. After a few minutes, the same fingers forced my head toward the window and I watched the same wisp of white smoke leave the apartment through the same window. The window closed slowly and the fingers let go of me. After what seemed like an hour, I finally got up to vomit up the fear in my stomach. Gina slept through the whole episode. I can't offer a logical explanation for what I believe to be some sort of supernatural occurrence.

We stayed there only a month, and decided to accept Gina's parents' offer to stay with them in Rocky Mount, North Carolina, while we got back on our feet financially. Shortly after we moved there, I realized that Gina and the rest of her family had never gotten along well, and the situation had become even worse since our marriage. My parents had gotten back together again, and soon after Gina and I arrived in Rocky Mount, they drove up to take us with them back to Riverdale, Georgia, a suburb south of Atlanta near Hartsfield International Airport. My father had transferred from Los Angeles to work for a small airline in

Atlanta, while my mother went to work for Lawyers' Title Insurance in downtown Atlanta. I went to work right away for Clayton County Hospital, where soon after we moved Gina gave birth to a beautiful little girl named April Leigh. The minute she was born I asked if she was deaf, but I knew it was too early to tell. I was terrified she would be deaf since both of us were deaf, but part of me was hoping she would be deaf. I wanted our baby to have the best education she could have, which I had gotten from a school for the deaf, but I also lived in fear that I might lose what residual hearing I still had. I wanted a child who could help us by answering the phone or just being there if we needed her.

Two years later, I was still working at the same job at the emergency room, but I hadn't given up my dream of working for the fire department. I happened to pick up a community college course booklet, where I discovered a course for emergency medical technicians sponsored by the Clayton County Fire Academy. Our son, Jason, was born that same year, and I decided that now was the time to move closer to my goal. After having worked in several hospitals, learning the medical terminology, and learning to feel comfortable in a medical atmosphere, I felt that I was ready to take the course. So far, no one suspected I was deaf, and I hoped that that would continue to be the case. Was I surprised! When I went down to the academy to sign up for the course, I ran into the first of many obstacles that I would face before becoming an emergency medical technician.

No sooner had I walked into the Fire Academy EMS Division Training Center than the secretary told me how hard she thought it would be for me to get into the class, since I couldn't hear very well. She almost didn't give me an application when I asked as nicely as I could if I could speak to the instructor. My story about having a cleft palate was getting old, and I think it was getting easier for a hearing person to spot my deafness.

It took several visits to the same fire academy to convince the instructor to give me a chance. He told me that if I failed the first test or any subsequent tests, I would be released, no questions asked. With a handshake and a nod, I started class two weeks later.

At about this same time, problems between Gina and me began to get worse, to the point that we agreed that we would both be better off if we got a divorce.

3
Becoming a Firefighter

To become a firefighter in the state of Georgia, one must meet rigorous physical standards that are determined by the state Firefighter Standards and Training Council. Because of my profound hearing loss, I did not meet the minimum standards, but only the chief and I knew that.

I had just completed the final eighteen hours of training required by the Clayton County Fire Academy, EMS Division, under the instruction of Sergeant Gus Swaney. The last three months of the year-long EMT course were nearly over, but I had a lot of "mopping up" to do, which involved working at local hospitals to observe and assist the emergency room staff. The last eighteen hours were spent mainly as a third rider on ambulance calls with the city of Morrow fire and rescue department. I was barely able to convince the chief to let me ride out with the others. He thought he had seen the last of me until I showed up asking about becoming a volunteer firefighter. After several meetings behind closed doors, and one instance of my begging him on my knees, he agreed to let me serve. He toyed with the idea of having me sign a waiver to protect himself and the department. The waiver would ensure that the department would not be held liable in the event I screwed up. As it turned out, I was never asked to sign the waiver. I don't think the chief even mentioned my disability to anyone above his chain of command.

Thus it was that I became a volunteer firefighter three months before I graduated from the Basic Emergency Medical Technician Course at the Clayton County Fire Academy. Before I came along, it was unheard of to have a deaf fireman within the ranks, and I was proud to be joining those ranks. In the United States, there are more than 1 million firefighters. On average, one firefighter is killed every three days and about half of the country's firefighters are injured each year. But it was a job that I thought would provide a deep sense of personal satisfaction. After all, I would be helping people in need. I was part of a tradition of public service that goes back more than 200 years. I attended every volunteer meeting and tried to learn as much as I could about the equipment used for fire suppression, auto extrication, and salvage operations.

As soon as the chief announced that I was joining the department, several of the other firefighters approached him and made their feelings known on this matter. Tension and resentment weighted heavily in the firehouse. At first the other guys would ignore me and refuse to acknowledge me as a fellow firefighter. If I protested their treatment of me, I was hastily reminded that if I couldn't stand the heat, then I could get the hell out of the kitchen. Most of the other firefighters would frequently use the words "deaf and dumb" to describe me. I knew that if I tried to retaliate, it would mean immediate dismissal. The chief often reminded me that I would have to earn the respect of the other men.

Earning their respect consisted of doing shit details like kitchen duty, cleaning the bathrooms, washing trucks, scrubbing hoses, doing paperwork, and much more. This was called tradition—the lowest-ranking man at the station invariably ended up doing jobs that the others didn't want to do. I once balked at a job order, saying that I was a volunteer and not getting paid. At that point one of the other firefighters, the biggest of them all, stepped forward, looked down at me, and said, "Better get that attitude changed, boy, if you want to work with us." It took me a while to realize that this intimidation served the purpose of testing me to see if I had what it took to be a fireman.

I continued to work as a volunteer fireman while I was employed as an EMT for a private ambulance service in Fulton County. At the station the other firefighters continued to enjoy making me the butt of their practical jokes, one of which involved placing a garbage can full of wet hay in the middle of the bunk room, igniting it, and evacuating the other guys while I was asleep. I woke up choking in a dark room. I had lost all sense of reality and direction. Up became down, down became up, and sideways was backward. I rolled over and fell to the floor and had enough sense to stay down and crawl out of the room into the bay where the fire trucks were kept. I had already dragged a booster hose off an engine to the bunkroom and was prepared to fight a fire and rescue the other guys when they came out of hiding laughing hysterically. Even I had to admit that that was a good one.

Another time they ganged up on me and handcuffed me to the metal bedpost in the bunkroom. They then stood around and laughed at me, calling me "deaf and stupid." This was just another test to see if I had what it took to be a fireman. They wanted to make sure that I could be trusted to back up another man. Just then the alarm went off and the fire dispatcher announced a fire call for a woman trapped. They all scrambled out of the room and headed for the trucks while I tried to disassemble the bedpost by taking off the mattress, sliding the box spring away, and unscrewing the head frame. I had every intention of going to the fire, even if I had to carry the bedpost with me. I managed to drag it halfway out of the bunkroom when the trucks began backing into the bay. I realized it was another false alarm when they all jumped out and started laughing at my expense.

Whenever the guys had a new joke to inflict they'd seek me out, and it wasn't long before I started to earn their respect, one by one. There were still a few hard-cores who flat-out refused to acknowledge me. One of them frequently assigned me to the ambulance to ride EMS for the twenty-four-hour shift, thinking that this was not what I wanted to do. Most of them avoided manning the rescue truck and would delegate that slot to the man with the least seniority. They didn't realize that this was my favorite kind of duty. It allowed me to run calls and sharpen my skills as a new EMT, and at the same time function as a firefighter during fire calls.

Through trial and error and learning to not repeat the same stupid mistakes, I gradually became a good firefighter. Fortunately, no one else was injured by my blunderings except myself.

The most deadly "mistake" I made was shooting a solid straight stream of water into the seat of a fire, sending burning embers and flames into a pocket of gas waiting for a source of ignition. The whole bedroom flashed into an instant ball of fire, forcing me and my partner to the floor. Realizing my horrible mistake, I switched to a wide fog and created a water umbrella of sorts to give us a measure of protection against the minor backdraft. I caught hell when we finally put a head on the fire and withdrew for the back-up team to mop up. "Couldn't ya hear it?" My partner was implying that a hearing firefighter could orient or aim for the crackling of a fire simply by listening, but I couldn't. And this was one situation when I couldn't rely on my eyes because locating a fire, already hidden and buried by the smoke, is impossible in most cases.

My solution was to shoot a stream into the ceiling and wait for the water to come back. If it was cold, I'd keep going deeper until I sent another shot into the smoke. If it came back hot, then I knew I was in the area. With luck, I could see some light through the smoke. When I couldn't, I simply became more suicidal and pushed myself until I could stick my hand into the very seat of the fire before I opened my nozzle. I was only homicidal when I took someone with me.

Most civilians have no earthly idea how dangerous firefighting is. They assume we just sit around, pull cats out of trees, chew snuff, and shoot the bull. Not hardly. If I was caught between sun up and sun down not doing anything, I could definitely expect to be given a reprimand and a shit detail, my least favorite being using my own toothbrush to scrub the bathroom floor. If I didn't find anything to do, I'd invent something to do. Often times, I was permitted to bury myself in books if all my chores were completed. Other times, I'd be all over the trucks to memorize the different tools used to fight fires, extricate auto accident victims, or for salvage and overhauling. The captain would often ask me for a specific piece of equipment and if I didn't know, then again I could expect another reprimand and to be sent to the bathroom.

No one can forget his first trauma call as a new EMT. Mine was in a warehouse section of the city's industrial area. Just as a forklift driver backed out of a trailer to unload material, the trailer rolled forward and the driver held out his arm to reach for safety. The forklift dropped between the loading dock and the trailer while the cage of the forklift amputated his arm. When I went to retrieve the severed arm from the break room of the warehouse, I was horrified to find the fingers still twitching.

On my twenty-first birthday I was rewarded with a full-time position as a firefighter. On my first call as a paid firefighter, we got a call for a fully involved house fire with a woman trapped inside. When we returned to quarters, I had earned my nickname, Catfish. The name originated then—I was pretty heavy at the time and my mustache made me look like a catfish after a dirty fire. I like to think that the name stuck because, like a channel catfish, I would do anything or go anywhere to get what I wanted.

The chief had told me that I needed to earn the respect of my fellow firefighters. After a while in the department, I realized that one way to force them to respect me was to learn as much, or more, than they knew. I spent hundreds of hours going to the fire academy.

Attending the fire academy was difficult for me, as I could not obtain an interpreter or a note-taker, nor could I hear and understand all of the classroom teaching. All of this was before passage of the Americans with Disabilities Act. I managed to adjust by placing myself in the front row in the classroom and taking notes based on what the instructor wrote on the blackboard. I was not about to ask the instructor to make allowances for me or to borrow notes from another student. I had to remind myself constantly that I was walking on eggshells and fighting tradition at the same time.

I was working as a paid firefighter for the Morrow fire department when I got my first OB call as an EMT. When we arrived, the mother was in labor and spotting blood badly. The father was on the phone with the doctor when we arrived, and he immediately handed me the phone when I walked in. After I identified myself, a doctor ordered me to transport the mother to a hospital fifty miles away, north of Atlanta. He told me that the mother was two weeks late and carrying twins. She was considered a high-risk patient because of her high blood pressure. I advised him that, given the nature of her condition, I wanted to transport her to the nearest hospital for stabilization. He threatened me with a lawsuit, saying he would have me brought before the State Board of Medical Examiners. He reminded me that under state law I was obligated to follow his medical orders. I feared the loss of my newly acquired EMT designation, so I agreed to take her to the hospital of the doctor's choice.

When we were about halfway there, in a driving thunderstorm, the woman began to experience horrible pain. She faded in and out of consciousness while her vital signs began to drop. Her water broke, and she began to bleed heavily. I decided to treat her in the same way as a trauma patient. The white sheet had turned dark red from the bleeding from her vagina. I decided that I would rather risk my certification as an EMT and take her to the nearest hospital. My partner, who was driving, was not familiar with any hospitals nearby and had directions only for the hospital we had been routed to. Meanwhile, I called our base hospital in Clayton County and asked to start an intravenous line of normal saline at a wide open rate. I started her on full oxygen with a rebreather bag while waiting for a response from the hospital. Permission was granted.

The bleeding became worse—large puddles of blood began to form on the floor of the patient compartment. I took the large trauma dressings kept in the cabinets and applied direct pressure in a fruitless effort to stanch the bleeding. Her vital signs fluctuated, and I had to adjust her IV constantly. I was prepared to try to deliver the twins just when we arrived at the hospital. The woman was quickly turned over to the emergency room. Before we left, the nurse informed us that the woman had had a set of stillborn twins and had later gone into cardiac arrest and died.

I have come to believe that if the academy embarked on the concept of using American Sign Language (ASL) as a means of communication in a fire ground situation, there would be less chance of miscommunication and misunderstanding. No one would have to strain and shout to be heard above the roar of fire and equipment. It could definitely benefit the attack teams inside a fire structure. Not surprisingly, no one has bought that concept.

My biggest advantage over my hearing colleagues during an actual fire call was my ability to understand a command by lipreading, although that worked only when we were outside a fire. Other firefighters were forced to make physical contact with each other, or at least be in close proximity to one another, in order to understand a command. I could read lips easily from any point in a fire ground situation. When I was inside a burning building, I had two rules that I had to strictly adhere to if I wanted to come back out alive. The first was to keep one hand on the hose at all times. Losing my grip on the hose could cost me my life, as the smoke might lead me astray and kill me if I ever lost my place. The other rule was to back my partner at all costs. After all, he was doing the same for me—trusting me with his life.

One of the difficulties that I encountered in a fire ground situation was that it was necessary for me to continuously feel the brass bell mounted on my air pack. A thirty-minute supply of compressed air, under normal firefighting conditions, is usually reduced to a safety margin of only ten minutes because of the physical exertion involved in search and rescue and in suppressing a fire. If my bell started to ring, I knew I had less than two minutes to get out by following the hose line back outside to safety. It was the most terrifying aspect of my firefighting career. That damn bell was my guardian angel and my protector. There were several occasions when I forgot to check my bell because I was preoccupied with searching for victims. It was terrifying to feel the bell stop ringing when I decided to check. The thought "I'm gonna be dead!" would be foremost in my mind. Reaching behind my air pack, I'd quickly purge the emergency valve for any remaining air in the bottle and take a deep breath.

Sometimes when I was only halfway out of the fire structure, the face piece would suddenly become an instrument of suffocation. Adrenaline would rip through me like a lightning bolt, and the urge to rip off the face mask was overwhelming. But somewhere in the back of my mind I could hear the instructor at the fire academy screaming at me that I'm dead, dead, dead, and dead if I so much as crack my mask. As my training kicked in, I would unscrew the hose from the regulator, jam it down inside my coat and underneath my armpit—this would give me just a few more seconds of air.

We were taught at the academy never to go inside on a search and rescue mission without a partner. This is a fine idea, but it only works in big cities. I was at the scene of a fire in a rural area when, after strapping the bulky air pack onto my back, I looked around to find someone to tell of my intent to go inside. There was no one around, except for a bunch of chickens with their feathers on fire, running from underneath the front porch. The fire academy also teaches you to use your right hand and right foot to maintain contact with the right side of the wall, while using your left hand and left leg to search for a body. It has been found that if you stay to the right at all times, you will eventually find your way out of a house. I entered the house, keeping to the right, and I tried to reach out as far as I could while inching along at the same time. When I came to a door frame, I made another right to follow the wall and continued on. I kept going until I realized that I was going around in circles inside a large closet. A couple of more turns failed to find the door frame that I had used to gain entrance. The air was fast becoming hotter, and the metal straps on my helmet were already getting uncomfortably warm. It was time to get out! I lost track of time, and kept checking my bell every few seconds. Paranoia was setting in, and I felt that I was losing control of myself.

I sat back against the wall and tried to figure a way out of this mess. My hearing aid felt awfully warm under the Nomex hood. I noticed that I couldn't hear any more of the fire crackling nearby or the trucks roaring outside—the smoke was becoming too thick for sound to penetrate. A few more circles continued to deny me an exit from the closet, and I decided that my fellow firefighters were going to find a dead deaf firefighter with his hand on his bell. I could almost hear them say, "Told ya, Chief! Deaf AND dumb!"

That was not about to happen. I had come a long way, I would never give them the satisfaction of saying that. I had worked hard at earning a reputation from the other volunteers, to the point of being considered either suicidal or homicidal when fighting fires. I suddenly remembered that I had failed to use a door wedge stored at the back of my helmet to keep the closet door propped open. The wedge is used to keep a door from slamming behind you and locking you in. I sensed that the fire was beginning to develop into the backdraft phase. Because of a shortage of manpower, ventilation had not been provided. In other words, smoke and gas could not escape into the atmosphere, and thus collected in the apex of the structure. I was just waiting for a spark to ignite the gas pocket while the expansion created a sucking motion on the hot air in the other parts of the house. I hadn't heard the door slam behind me when I entered the walk-in closet.

All I had to do now was locate the door frame, but there was none. Pushing, shoving, and banging on all four walls only convinced me that I was surrounded by four solid walls with no door. Meanwhile, the backup fire companies had laid out a line through the front door and attacked the fire in the kitchen, while more firefighters broke windows and cut a hole into the roof so that smoke and gas could escape. As I became resigned to my fate, one of the four walls somehow became the door. The fresh stream of water had begun to cool the house down enough to eliminate the potential for a backdraft, thus allowing my escape. I meekly joined the rest of the guys on the line and acted like nothing out of the ordinary had happened.

I took a number of courses designed to hone my skills as a firefighter. A course in explosives taught us the basics of how to make bombs—including what materials were needed to build different types of firebombs and explosives. I learned that a Mason jar, three drops of gasoline, and a cutout of the diamonds from a stack of playing cards could make a bomb that would make a nice five-inch hole in a brick wall. The same instructor for this course showed us how to put out a small fire with a bucket of gasoline to prove a point. He also described ways of using a simple butane lighter to blow up a car. I have since then seen firsthand the deadly effects of the butane lighter. In one case a lighter was left on the dashboard and the sun caused it to ignite. Another involved a welder whose butane lighter exploded in his pocket.

I learned that blowing up a car does not require explosives or special equipment. A car's electrical system and half a tank of gas can be an explosive combination. What most people don't realize is that a half tank of gasoline is more explosive than a full tank—the gas fumes provide the flash point for the explosion, not the gasoline itself. A full tank of gasoline leaves no room for fumes to accumulate.

I consider the smoke diver course my biggest failure, and it had nothing to do with my hearing loss. I can only compare this course to something like the navy SEAL program, where more than half the class failed during the first or second day of the forty-hour course. I made it to the third day, when I failed by taking off my oxygen mask to vomit. That was a big no-no, and the instructor couldn't wait to slam his face into mine to scream that I was dead. If a firefighter removes his mask to vomit while inside a burning building, he will very likely end up dead from the first blast of super-heated gas and smoke. The correct procedure is to keep the mask on, no matter what, and let the hose connected to the face mask drain the vomitus.

As part of this same course I learned to appreciate myself more than I ever had before. They covered my face mask with duct tape to simulate a heavy smoke condition during a search and rescue operation. I was already deaf, and at that point I became blind as well when I entered the tower. The inside of the tower, from the bottom floor to the top, consisted of hundreds of pallets resembling miniature hall-ways and doors leading to nowhere. I was sure that the other students could rely on their hearing to lead them through the obstacles, while I was forced to depend on my sense of touch and direction. That became a deadly com-bination when I suddenly fell forward into a hole full of water. I later found out that it was only three feet deep by four feet square, but at the time I was sure that it was the Atlantic Ocean.

The next day, in the same tower, we simulated another search and rescue (no masks allowed) with a hot fire cook-ing off a stack of wooden pallets in the basement. There'd be five different hoses snaking into the building and going in all directions. The hoses were horribly intertwined and twisted in some places. The object of the exercise was for a student to carry two air bottles, pick a hose, and then find the other end of the chosen hose. Without an air pack and a mask, a student would try to go as far as he could before taking a fresh breath of compressed air from the bottle. In short order, the first bottle would be emptied, and the stu-dent would be forced to use the second bottle to reach his destination. I failed, and backed out in disgrace. It was the first time I could not complete a course at the fire acad-emy, and I was taking it pretty hard. The fire chief reas-sured me when he said, "None of the other guys will even get off their fat asses to take this class." That made me feel better. I had tried something harder than the guys back at the station.

The academy also provided a course in defensive driv-ing—the Emergency Vehicle Operation Course, known as EVOC for short. Again, more than half the students who signed up for the course failed on the first and second day of a forty-hour week. I came out on top at the end, with a record of backing a vehicle through a lane of more than 400 safety cones without knocking down a single one. One of the instructors, a former state trooper, made me repeat this feat several times before he was convinced that I had broken his own record of three minutes and ten seconds by one full minute. It wasn't so much the course agenda that caused students to fail as it was the instructors themselves who tried to intimidate them by screaming, threatening, and provoking. I was glad to be deaf in this class. I could ignore the instructor who was riding shotgun with me by turning off my hearing aid without letting him know. That didn't stop him from hitting me on the NASCAR-approved helmet and poking his finger into my face during a test. These guys had to have been as mean as Marine Corps drill instructors.

Included in the curriculum of this course were such topics as how to correct a vehicle during a skid or a hydroplaning situation. Another section of the course involved learning to brake suddenly whenever they threw out a cardboard cutout of a human figure or how to run through an intersection safely. We were each allowed to have three human kills before getting kicked out of the class. I ran down a mother and her baby in a carriage, which counted as two. Another part of the course involved "curb-jumping," in which students learned to jump curbs at 80 miles per hour to simulate an emergency run. There were lots of tires blown and rims broken to pieces by improper jumping. The tires had to be at a certain angle in order to successfully jump a one-foot curb with either two or four wheels.

To anticipate braking problems, the instructor had at his disposal a switch he could depress to turn off the brake and force the student driver to use other options to slow the car down. A number of students had the habit of using the left foot to brake, which always pissed off the instructors. They solved that problem by screwing an eye bolt onto the floorboard of the left side of the brake pedal. If the instructor caught the student using the left foot to brake, he'd personally tie the student's shoelaces to the eye bolt to force him to use the right foot. This was the most fun I had during all my years at the academy. The driving instructors never realized that I was deaf. They assumed that I had a cleft palate instead.

By the end of my firefighting career I had earned numerous certifications, ranging from basic and advanced firefighting through courses in hazardous materials, aircraft rescue, and tactical rope rescue. I found that every certification and license earned me another notch of respect from my fellow firefighters. My superior officers would gradually delegate more and more responsibility, and I came to hear less and less the term "deaf and dumb."

4

War Stories

On March 28, 1982, I received my certification and my new Emergency Medical Technician number from the state of Georgia. I had had serious doubts about whether I had passed the course. It had taken nine long months, and as it was, I passed the course by only one point. I knew I had flunked the obstetrical section of the state board examination, but the trauma and medical sections of the test had saved me. Ironically I ended up handling twenty-one full or assisted deliveries.

It never occurred to me during my career that I was possibly the country's only deaf firefighter and emergency medical technician with a true deaf education. I became an artist at hiding my disability. I would "lose" it when reporting for duty, whether at the fire station or the hospital, and reclaim it when I came home.

Only a few people, including the fire chief and my partners, were aware of my deaf-educated background and the severity of my hearing loss, though I wore bilateral hearing aids, that allowed me to hear and understand most people's speech. I had to alter my application in order to be considered for an EMT position with Grady Memorial Hospital in downtown Atlanta. I also worked part-time for Henry County Fire and Rescue, south of Atlanta.

On my application to Grady, I abbreviated the Eastern North Carolina School for the Deaf as ENCSD, and refused to sign the Handicapped Statement. Any references to the word *deaf* were eliminated. During the first of several interviews, I hid my hearing aids under my ear-length hair, which I had grown long specifically for that purpose, and relied heavily on my lipreading ability. I spoke as little as possible, hoping that no one would not notice my speech impediment.

After several grueling interviews with the hospital's training department, I was hired. The knowledge that there was a deaf EMT within the ranks was not reassuring to the other EMTs. In fact, I myself was scared shitless. It was not so much that I was scared of them, but that I was scared for myself and what I was doing. The training department at the hospital was responsible for screening selected applicants after subjecting them to numerous tests designed to weed out those lacking the skills required. I maintained the "listen, learn, and say as little as possible" mode while going through the application process.

Thirty days later, Grady Hospital called and told me to report for duty on January 3, 1985. Since the establishment of the ambulance department in 1896, we were attending the first organized mass orientation designed by the hospital's training department. There were more than twenty of us in the three-month training program, and when we "graduated," fifteen of us remained.

My disability was complicated by prejudice and discrimination from the very people I was trying to help. But these were the least of my worries. I wondered about my ability to survive on the streets. I had heard so many things about Grady, like the fact that the average employee turnover rate was six months. Although I did meet some people who had been there for eight or ten years, they were guys who had gotten off the streets to work for the training department.

I found that working for Grady EMS was extremely hazardous to my health for the first six months of my employment. My immune system completely shut down, and every known virus and infection, such as strep, colds, flu, and respiratory infection, seemed to gravitate toward me. I thought that I had caught just about everything that I could think of, when my immune system finally seemed to build up a high tolerance against infection. It was rare for me to get sick, except for an occasional hangover or a stomach problem from a bad hamburger. The only other thing that ever made me sick after that, although it was effective in the long run, was the flu shot.

One of my first partners, a former Marine Corps veteran who served as a medic in Vietnam, claimed that two years on the streets working the graveyard shift was equal to one year in Vietnam. The people in certain parts of town would prepare a nightly defensive perimeter that would make an army firebase commander proud. Common hazards included razor blades embedded in handrails, nails in floors, firearms rigged to shoot through doors, and pricked fingers from needles found in patients' pockets.

I quickly learned a few rules for survival on the streets:

— Always wear a bulletproof vest.
— Watch your partner's back and have your partner do the same for you.
— Keep a weapon (out of sight of the supervisors, of course).
— Never let people approach your ambulance door.
— Never hang your arm out the window. (I've had several

watches stolen by runners who snatch watches off people as they're waiting at a traffic light.)
— Never, never stand in front of a door when knocking.

I always kept my maglight at arm's length away from my body in case I got shot at. People would tend to shoot at the source of the light. I learned to check everyone for concealed weapons. If anyone complained, I would just tell them that I was checking for injuries.

The most important survival technique for me was to make damn sure that there were sufficient batteries for my hearing aid. I owned two, but refused to wear more than one at a time. That way, if one should be damaged, I would have a backup. I needed all of my residual hearing in order to keep myself alive.

There were numerous drawbacks to wearing a hearing aid. During the summer I had to keep a terry cloth towel around my neck to keep the sweat from shorting out my hearing aid. Every week I visited the hearing aid shop on Peachtree Street to have it completely overhauled, which involved cleaning the mechanism and replacing the tube. Bending over a patient presented another problem. The hearing aid would fall forward and hang by its tube. I fixed that by using skin tape to keep the hearing aid from falling off.

I worried constantly about getting hit in the head. I was injured several times from violent patients slapping me in the ear that held my hearing aid. The pain was excruciating, sometimes resulting in brief loss of consciousness. Whenever I anticipated a confrontation, I learned to quickly remove my hearing aid and pocket it in a pouch snapped to a gunbelt that I had purchased for that purpose.

I found that taking out my hearing aid in front of a

suicidal patient and fiddling with it could calm a tense situation in no time at all, thus buying me the time I needed to talk the patient into changing his mind. Using sign language and trying to communicate with my obvious speech impediment became a favorite tactic of mine. I found that it worked wonders with demented patients, too. I haven't yet figured out why, but it was always important to me that patients understand that I had a disability.

Once I was called in when a man was holding a gun to his head. I approached his bedroom door and stopped to take out my hearing aid. I asked the man, "Do you have a hearing aid battery lying around here? I sure could use one. I'm deaf as that post out there." I could see him slacken his hold on the gun. The long rusted barrel rested on his collarbone and the large hammer was pulled back. He looked around and said he thought they might be in the nightstand. He leaned over slightly and looked past his wife, who lay on the bed beside him. She was a victim of Alzheimer's disease and was completely unaware of her surroundings. I could see this turning into a classic murder-suicide, and I prayed that I had stopped it in time.

I walked over slowly to the opposite side of the bed and opened the drawer to retrieve a pack of batteries. "Can I have a pack?" I asked. "I'll come back and pay you for it." He said that I could have them. While changing the batteries, I sat on the bed next to the man's wife and prepared to put my hearing aid back into my ear. "So, I feel better now. I can hear again. If you told me your name, I'm sorry, I must have missed it. What is it?"

The old man sensed that he had found someone who would listen to him. He poured out his troubles and told me of night after night without seeing the light at the end of the tunnel. He had had a hell of a time trying to get people or services to help him care for his wife. He had come to the end of his rope and said he planned to kill his wife and then himself. His son just happened to come by and find his father with a gun in his hand. He called 911.

The man took my advice to come down to the hospital after I promised that I would help him get help for his situation. Unfortunately, my unit was called out on another emergency and I didn't see the old man again until a few months later, when we responded to a man shot in Cabbagetown, a community on the southeast side of the city. It was the same house and the same old man with his wife beside him in bed. He had shot himself in the mouth. I was mad as hell at myself for not following through on my promise to the old man. He was pronounced dead on arrival.

Lipreading became a vital tool for me, and I learned to use it with help from my hearing aid. When driving, my partner and I developed a system based primarily on our own form of ASL using the rearview mirror. My partner would "talk" to me by holding a thumb up and then two fingers to indicate a Code 2 run (lights only). If he wanted me to call ahead to the hospital, he would pretend to hold a phone to his ear, and then hold up five fingers to indicate the hospital frequency. I often had to read his mind to fill in the blanks. If he really felt that he needed to talk to me, he would come forward and talk directly in my ear.

In many of the calls that I went on, my deafness never became an issue, neither for the patients nor for my partner. Some of the details of these "war stories" may be gruesome to the uninitiated, but I am only trying to convey the reality of life as an EMT.

My deafness did become an issue once when an APD officer responded with me and my partner to a gunshot call and wanted to arrest me for suspicion of DUI. He had heard me questioning the patient and determined, unaware of my speech impediment, that I was under the influence of alcohol. Without regard to the man bleeding from three gunshot wounds, the officer poked me with his nightstick and ordered me outside. I had no idea why he was poking me, so I proceeded to work the call. A few minutes later he prodded me a little harder and ordered me outside. This prompted me to stop, stand up with blood dripping from my latex gloves and order him outside to control the gathering crowd. As far as the law is concerned, once APD secured the scene and rendered it safe for us to take control, we were in charge. The patient is legally in the EMT's care until such time as the responsibility has been signed over to another, more highly trained paramedic or to a hospital. I reminded the cop, who stood bewildered, that I was still in charge and if he wanted to talk to me, he could wait till after transport.

This did not deter him from cuffing me, in front of everybody, to lead me away to his squad car. Meanwhile, my partner was literally screaming at the officer and radioing the supervisor for another truck for assistance. The officer who placed me under arrest explained to his watch commander and the EMS supervisor that my speech was slurred and I refused to comply with his request. When told that I was deaf and I had a speech impediment, he immediately became defensive, demanding to know why a deaf EMT was on the street.

Most of the time, the EMTs and the cops had a pretty good working relationship. We all looked forward to the late night "choirs" at Grant Park. We'd show up after our shifts to kill the stress generated by working on the streets. Kegs of beer stacked on the sidewalk, hookers brought in by off-duty cops, and the aroma of beer, whiskey, and reefer kept the "volunteer" lookouts (uniformed officers on duty) stationed at the entrance of the park to keep unwanted guests out. The EMTs knew better than to mess with the hookers, so the girls went after drunken cops and rolled them for their wallets.

The next day, many of us would remember only the first twenty minutes of the party or the first twenty shots of Southern Comfort, whichever came first, and nothing else. To kill the hangovers, we breathed 100 percent oxygen and sneaked a few of the B-12 multivitamin shots from the drug box. One particular morning I asked my partner where he was when he came to that morning. He boasted that he was home in bed, but he couldn't imagine how he could have possibly driven all the way home. Me? I woke up on the patio steps of an ex-girlfriend who lived 120 miles north, almost to the state line. Thank God I woke up before she found me there. I left as quietly as I could, my head feeling like it was going to fall in pieces to the ground from the pounding inside.

An electrician had been electrocuted in an accident at the General Motors Lakewood assembly plant. The victim had been working alone in the plant's paint shop when the accident occurred, sometime before midnight. He was changing sockets for fluorescent light fixtures when he apparently clipped onto a live wire. He was discovered by a coworker after the lights in the plant had flickered on and off several times. After we arrived, we simply followed our noses. The victim, who was a journeyman electrician and father of two children, had worked for GM for nine years. He lay stiff as a board on a stretcher with his feet fused together. The workers had brought him to the nurse's station to await our arrival. His belt buckle had become a pool of molten metal, and the stench of burned tissues and involuntary bowel movement made us gag and gasp for fresh air. A charge of more than 20,000 volts had traveled from his right thumb, down his arm, to explode inside his chest cavity.

The explosion had created a hole the size of a basketball from one armpit to the other, such that I could see my partner through the hole when we tried to lift the man for examination. There was no evidence of heart and lungs. The organs had simply vanished. Departmental policy required that, whenever civilians were at the scene, we had to initiate life support efforts for the victim. I felt very foolish sticking an EOA (esophageal obturator airway) down the victim's airway to insert a tube for breathing, and then compressing a useless ambubag. The man's coworkers were horrified to see the tip of the EOA, with balloon inflated to secure the tube in place, dangling in plain view inside the chest.

Few of my calls were more traumatic for me than an accident that occurred on Interstate 285 near the Clayton County line. A truck driver had picked up a young female hitchhiker, seven months pregnant, at a rest area. It was nearly four in the morning when the truck driver fell asleep at the wheel and veered off to rear-end another truck parked in the emergency lane. When we arrived, my partner and I had a hard time believing what we were seeing. The cab of the truck containing the woman and driver resembled a smashed beer can, with the huge engine pushed through the bulkwall of the trailer. The driver escaped with a broken arm, but the female hitchhiker was dead. When we realized that the woman was pregnant, we tried to determine the status of the fetus. My partner, an advanced EMT, discovered to our horror a strong heartbeat when he placed his stethoscope on the left side of the dead woman's abdomen. We could see that it would be impossible to remove the woman from the wreckage without amputating both her legs, and my partner wanted to perform an emergency Caesarean on the spot. I implored him to maintain life support on the mother by doing cardiopulmonary resuscitation (CPR) until I could get a doctor from Grady Hospital on the radio.

While I was on the radio waiting for a response from the emergency room, I could see my partner getting out his pocketknife and heating it with a lighter. He still had not begun CPR. Just as I thought he would, the doctor instructed us to maintain CPR and life support until he could get to the scene. I told my partner to stand by, and I screamed out the back of the truck for him not to do a cutdown. I had been pleading with him to wait for authorization. As soon as I told him that the doctor was on the way, he jumped down and walked away. I knew then that it was too late. I got back on the radio and told the doctor to disregard. My partner wouldn't speak to me again for the next few weeks.

A twenty-seven-year-old man was killed, and a female passenger severely injured, when their car, traveling at more than 120 miles per hour, struck a median wall on Interstate 285 on the west side of Atlanta and overturned. The car had rolled, ejecting both the driver and the passenger, more than 450 feet before it finally came to rest upright in the middle of the northbound lanes. When we arrived, we found the driver pinned face down on the asphalt with the transmission casing resting on the back of his neck. There was a large pool of vomitus, an indication of head trauma and of the fact that he may have lived for a few minutes afterward. His right leg, broken in a dozen places and twisted like a rubber band, was still held tight to the side of the driver's door and anchored securely with his seat belt. Apparently on the last roll, he ejected and his leg remained wrapped in the seat belt.

The female passenger was not discovered until a passerby drove past the accident. She had been deposited against a bridge median wall, about another 120 feet ahead of the car. She was barely alive, having suffered massive internal injuries as well as trauma, including partial amputation of the right leg at the hip joint. We eventually determined that the driver had been en route to his home in Cherokee County from a drag race and that the car he had wrecked was the very same used in the drag race. The most unusual thing about the accident was the lack of debris in the roadway—no glass, no metal shards, no tools, nor any other indications of a wreck. Upon examining the car, we found that it had been stripped of everything except the driver's seat. There were roll bars mounted and a nitrous oxide bottle on the floorboard.

We responded on a help call with the fire department to a residential high-rise. My partner and I were taken by complete surprise when we heard a woman screaming at the top of her lungs. I kicked the door in and could smell the familiar odor of burned flesh as I noticed a haze of bluish smoke lingering in the room. The woman continued to scream in terror. We found her tied to a bed with neckties and belts. Her vagina had been set on fire with lighter fluid by a male customer who was paying for sex. Apparently he hadn't been pleased with the service.

Four firefighters were severely injured, one enough to be admitted to the burn unit at Grady Memorial Hospital, when they were trapped in a burning building at Edgewood and Jackson Streets. The burning four-story brick building was once the property of the Ebenezer Baptist Church, home church of the late Dr. Martin Luther King and his family, before it was sold to the city. It had been neglected since then, and it had become a perfect haven for homeless people.

A police helicopter monitoring the fire lost power and made a forced landing in a kudzu patch separating the building from the church. The two pilots were slightly injured, their dignity severely damaged and egos deflated. Another police officer who was directing traffic away from the fire collapsed after breathing in too much of the smoke. All three were transported to Grady and treated.

My partner and I were the first EMTs on the scene. When I called us out to the EMS dispatcher, I heard someone say something in response and my partner started to laugh. "Man back at the office wants me to put a dogleash on you." Very funny!

Amazingly, there were no firefighters to be seen. I walked over to the other side of the firetruck, fully expecting to see the engineer working on the pump panel, but no one was there. I followed the hoseline pulled from the bed of the truck to the front door. Stooping down on one knee beside the door while trying to avoid the heat blasting through, I tried to call out to the fireman inside. I could hear nothing but the roar of the fire. I tugged on the hoseline and was shocked beyond belief—no water pressure! That meant no water. They must've been deep inside.

It was about this time that I could hear the sirens wailing through the streets as the city of Atlanta's finest began to converge upon the fireground. I ran around to the side of the building and noticed a gloved hand sticking out a metal-barred window. It was on fire. I was horrified. Two more smoking gloved hands broke through the remaining glass. Smoke poured out the broken holes in the chicken-wired window while pieces of the burning gloves fell to the sidewalk. I stood there and there was nothing I could do to help them. The rage inside me exploded and the anger built rapidly as I jumped to grab onto the metal bars. With my two feet planted firmly on the brick wall, I tugged with all my might, praying that the bolts had long rusted away, at least just enough for me to bend a corner. It was too secure. Some bystanders rushed over to help me. We formed a pyramid, but it was utterly hopeless. The hands disappeared back inside. My heart sank as the pyramid broke up. I was sure then that everyone inside was already dead.

Evidently, half of the Atlanta Fire Department responded very quickly, and they were able to pry the bars off to pull the people trapped inside to safety. God was with them. Apparently, the team had entered the building and walked toward the back of the house. On the way, they put out a fire on a discarded rotting mattress and continued forward. A gust of air re-ignited the mattress and the fire grew rapidly. The flames roared across the old wooden oil-soaked floor to burn through the single two-and-a-half inch hoseline. The team was trapped by a wall of fire with no water.

During salvage and overhauling, four homeless men were found, burned beyond recognition. I noticed one of the bodies had vaporized leaving a faint outline of the man in chalk. The only physical remains left was a pile of large intestines, still smoldering like sausages in a frying pan.

We responded to a sick call at a liquor store on Simpson Avenue. It was raining and getting on toward morning when we pulled into the parking lot and noticed a white man holding on to the brick wall for support. He could just barely wave us over before he had to grab the wall again. "What's wrong, bud?" my partner asked.

I didn't notice anything unusual, except that he stank to high heaven and wore alcohol-soaked clothing. "What's wrong? Are you sick or something?" we asked again. The man dropped one hand and weakly pointed to his ass.

"It hurt real bad," he managed to say. He was out of breath again.

"Are you having trouble breathing?" we asked. He slowly shook his head. "Are you a drinking man?" my partner asked with concern. We felt that he was probably a harmless old man who had wandered in off the interstate.

I went back to the truck and retrieved the stretcher to wheel it back to the brick wall. "Here. Lie down on this bed. We'll take you to Grady and get you fixed up, okay?"

"Ooh . . . I'm VA. Can I go to the VA hospital?" he asked.

"Sure," we said, "no problem. Do you have a VA card on you?"

He merely nodded and pointed to his ass again to indicate that it was in his wallet. "Don't worry about it. I'll get it for you," I said. I reached for his back pocket and was looking for a wallet when I felt something wet and sticky with an unusual bulge that reached down the back of his right pantsleg. "Hey, give me your snipper," I said to my partner. "I want to cut his pants off."

The old man protested weakly and told us he didn't have any more pants to wear. We assured him that the VA hospital would provide for him. Just as I cut past the back pocket, I saw it. "Oooh shit! I've heard of partial prolapse, but this one looks like a total." I jumped on the radio and called the ER. "Grady Unit to SEC (Surgical Emergency Clinic), I've got a total prolapse of the rectum. Alcohol abuse evident."

The man died later at the VA hospital. It turned out that he had been a World War II hero and nobody cared. The total prolapse indicated that his whole rectum had turned inside out and hung like a rock formation found in caves.

I have seen a lot of rapes, but only one still sticks like molasses in my mind. When we arrived on the scene there were fire trucks and what looked like half the damn police department. I sent my partner to get the scoop from one of the officers on the scene, while I went directly to the victim to render assistance. Several police officers and neighbors had gathered at the front door of the victim's house, but no one could get near the rape victim without throwing her into another fit of violence. She was completely naked and had destroyed the furniture in the living room. She huddled in the far dark corner of the room, crying like a small child.

I closed the front door and sat on a chair at the opposite end of the room and waited a moment or two. The room was illuminated only by crazy patterns of blue, white, and red lights flashing from the equipment waiting outside. Every now and then I could see her tear-streaked contorted face in the lights of the emergency vehicles. She continued to huddle in the corner but, after a few more quiet moments, began to settle down enough to stop shaking. She hugged herself while trying to hide her nudity. I realized then what she was trying to do, so I took a light baby blanket off the couch and laid it before her on the floor before going back to my seat.

After what seemed like an eternity, she got up off the floor and walked over to the couch and wrapped herself tight with the blanket I offered her. I got up slowly and offered my hand. She took it, and I walked her through the amazed crowd of police officers, firefighters, and neighbors to the back of my truck. During transport to Georgia Baptist Hospital, I decided to dim the interior lights of the ambulance and sit quietly in the captain's chair directly behind her. We still hadn't said a word to one another.

When we were almost halfway to the hospital, she began to reenact the actual rape while on the stretcher. She moaned and began to thrash about on the bed. She appeared to be involuntarily restrained by unseen hands. Her eyes were wide and her face was shoved to one side and held down firmly. Her scream was being muffled with intermittent pleas to stop. I swear on my grandfather's grave that I could see the foam stretcher being compressed and released as if somebody were indeed on top of her.

Fear held me with icy fingers and kept me pinned to the chair. All I could do was watch with horrified fascination. I could almost see the guy on top of her, raping her with brute force before my very eyes. As soon as it started, it was over. She lay limp and sweating as if in complete exhaustion. "Are you all right?" I asked in almost a whisper. She reached down between her legs and then sat straight up on the bed to look me dead in the eye. She then handed me a used condom and smiled an evil smile. Her mind had snapped.

My partner later explained to me that she had been visiting from California and staying with a girlfriend. After she had gone to bed, her girlfriend had gone next door to talk to another friend. An ex-convict, just released from jail, had been waiting in the bushes with an eye on the pretty young lady who lay asleep in the apartment. She had come to Georgia after having been raped in California just days before.

I got my ass chewed out royally by the head honcho of the emergency room, who reminded me at the same time that I had no business being a deaf EMT. The doctor was a regular asshole around the emergency room and considered himself quite proficient at judging other people. The problem was that I had just brought in a hooker who was supposedly shot, but I couldn't find any gunshot wounds on her. I had completely stripped her of her clothes, which hadn't amounted to much, while a fire department medic was doing chest compression.

When we first arrived on the scene, everybody in the neighborhood said that Missouri, the patient, had been shot by her pimp. I saw no blood, bullet holes, or any other indication of a gunshot wound and decided to work it as a medical case and treat for cardiac arrest from unknown causes. At the ER, I informed the nurse of the gunshot story by the witnesses, but we were still unable to locate any gunshot wounds. During the work-up of the patient, a nurse was attaching EKG pads to the chest when she lifted one of her breasts and discovered a tiny bullet hole. Missouri had been running when she was shot with a .22-caliber bullet. The slug had entered her chest just as her unsupported left breast was bouncing. The exit wound was finally located a mere half-inch from the rectum.

A woman called 911 to ask that someone from Grady be sent to her son's apartment at the Martin Luther King, Jr., Building, next to the Grady Homes Housing Project. She had been trying to get her son to come to the door or an-swer the phone all weekend. She was worried because he was diabetic.

We weren't too concerned about the call—it was the type classified as a "welfare check"—so we stopped to grab a sandwich before heading out to the location. Two officers from the Atlanta Police Department had already gone up-stairs and were heading back downstairs with puke on the front of their uniform shirts.

"What is it now?" I asked. I hated surprises. One of them had just caught his breath.

"Dead, dead, dead, and dead!" he said.

I was instantly relieved. "Oh cool," I said. "You came and you saw. We are gone, since you guys can handle this."

"Not so fast, Catfish," one of the cops said. "We came and we didn't see."

Damn, I thought to myself, and turned around. "Guess you will have to go and confirm, huh?" the cop said.

I had to ask, hoping against hope, "How do you know he's dead?"

"Ooh, you will know just as soon as you get off the el-evator. While you're up there, get us a name too."

This time I laughed. "Of course now you guys have to come with us."

"Why?" they asked in unison.

"Because I'm requesting it." I held out my hand for them to lead the way. "You first," I said.

The second cop didn't want to go. "We'll sign your trip report and call funeral for you. I need to get back to my last call."

I took out my portable radio. "I'll just call dispatch and ask for APD and they'll just call you right back. So come on. Let's get this over with."

On the elevator up to the seventh floor, both of the cops took out their handkerchiefs and clamped them to the mouths and noses. I turned to my partner and tried to suppress a snicker and a smile. The doors opened and I screamed, "Close the doors!!! Oooo God!" My eyeballs felt like they were going to split down the middle. Tears cascaded down my face. The stench of death blowing in through the doors robbed my breath. We all gagged and dry-heaved to the first-floor lobby and ran outside for fresh air. The cops were cursing. "That's it! I don't get paid to do shit like this!"

I called the fire department to send a ladder truck to our location. After they arrived I borrowed an airpack breathing device and went back upstairs using the same elevator. By this time, the building manager had arrived, and she accompanied me to the dead man's apartment.

"How can you breathe this?" I asked her. It didn't seem to bother her. The other residents on the seventh floor were going about their daily business as if nothing out of the ordinary were happening.

We both turned down the hallway and headed for the dead man's apartment. I could have sworn that I could see the door breathing in and out. The building manager asked, "Is this the door? He's a mute, you know. He just moved here last week." I wasn't in the mood to care whether the man was deaf or not. The stench of death permeated my facepiece, forcing me to open the emergency valve to purge more fresh air for me to breathe. The manager took out her set of keys and began looking for a master key. She had to stop several times to look for the right pair of glasses that spilled forth from her apron pocket. I was getting sicker by the second and was on the verge of vomiting in my own face mask.

She finally found the key, opened the door, and stepped back. Finally it hit her. She vomited on the wall and on herself. I poked my head inside the hot and raunchy apartment and could see him on his bed with his arms and legs stretched like an upside-down dead spider. His face had ballooned while his tongue stuck out between his lips. That was enough for me. I was convinced that he was dead, dead, dead, and double-dead.

Things were real slow, and I was talking to a brand new cop who had just been assigned to his first car after graduating from the academy. It was almost three in the morning, and the usual bunch of cops and EMTs had gathered in the parking lot of the Kroger on Stewart Avenue (hooker's alley) to shoot the bull and eat supper.

"Damn, man," I said to him, "they got you hot smack in the combat zone first thing, huh?"

He started to say something when he got a call about a man with a gun, just down the street from where we were standing. "Well, gotta go," he said. "I might be callin' ya." He laughed as he pulled away with blue lights flashing. I went back to my truck to find my supper.

In just a few minutes, a call was dispatched to us for the same address that the cop had gone on. A man had been shot. "Radio," I shouted, "advise if APD is the victim."

"Negative," was the reply. "Perpetrator shot by APD. No further information. Rescue en route to assist. Use extreme caution upon arrival."

When we pulled up to the address, a Hispanic female was waving us frantically to her door, shouting in Spanish and pointing down the dark hallway. My partner took her away while I took up position next to the doorway and held out my flashlight. "Grady here," I shouted. "APD, are you in there?"

"Yeah," was the reply. "I shot him. I don't know if I killed him. I can't move. I need backup. I gotta keep him covered." The new cop had gone in without his radio and without waiting for backup to arrive.

He stood there in a combat stance while keeping his service revolver pointed to the male Hispanic who lay back against a small closet. He was still pointing the shotgun, with his finger still in the trigger guard. With extreme caution I crept slowly past the cop to get a closer look. "I can't tell," I said. "I don't know if he's dead or not." I backed up a little, out of his range of fire. "You keep that weapon on him. Shoot if he so much as breathes." The cop responded by pulling back the hammer and taking a sharper bead on the man.

I stayed out of his line of fire and crawled on my hands and knees to the closet where the man lay. Reaching inside, I gently pulled his trigger finger, ever so softly, away from the trigger guard of the shotgun. The cop moved forward, weapon still pointed, and took the shotgun away. I reached up to the carotid artery and felt for a pulse. "Yeah, he's dead," I said.

The cop suddenly relaxed and sat back down on the flimsy bed. "Hell of a way to start the shift, huh?" He tried to find some humor in all this.

I just shook my head. "Yeah, well," I said, "you mean it's a hell of a way to start a career."

Incidentally, the shotgun was found to be unloaded.

A five-year-old kid was playing with a razor blade, cutting up a bar of soap in the bathroom, when his buddies called him to play. He put the blade in his jeans pocket, ran down-stairs, and tripped on the doorstep. He fell and got up to run before he stopped and noticed a tremendous amount of blood cascading down both his legs and onto the side-walk. He screamed and ran home to his mother. We arrived to find that half of the boy's penis had been severed. Once I found the other end of the severed penis, we promptly iced it down for immediate transport to the hospital. I never did do a follow-up on this boy, but I felt like I'd been kicked in the groin after this call!

Two brothers had tried to beat each other senseless after a day-long drunk. Just before APD arrived to break up the fight, one of the brothers bit off the other's entire upper lip and mustache. I wanted to retrieve the "item" for pos-sible reattachment by emergency surgery. I asked the offend-ing brother, who had already been placed under arrest and was sitting in the back of a patrol car, if he could please tell me where he had spit it out. His face was smeared with blood as he smiled at me, licked his lips, and burped.

A family of four—mother, father, son, and baby daughter—had just left Thanksgiving dinner with some close friends when the car they were riding in crossed the center line to smash head-on into another car. The father's head was found 150 feet from the accident, and the bodies of his wife and son remained trapped in the wreckage, but there was no baby. We were not aware of the infant until a car pulled up, and out jumped a hysterical man and his wife.

"They just left us. I heard the crash," the man said.

His wife asked, "Where's the baby?"

We conducted a search by working our way back toward

the wreck from where the man's head had been found. We found no baby. We tried again, looking more closely. Again, nothing.

As I was doing some paperwork, using one of the wrecked cars as a platform, a large drop splattered on my arm. I thought it had started to rain until I flicked on my maglight and noticed that my arm was red and sticky. I looked up slowly, only to find the missing baby impaled on a short tree limb.

I was particularly fond of a young mother who traveled in an old mountain jalopy, a once proud 1957 Buick, across the county to find me and thank me from the bottom of her heart for saving the life of her two-year-old baby girl.

It was that one call that took all the energy, skills learned from Grady, and concentration I had to work on the little girl. She had just finished eating a slice of pizza when she wandered outside and fell into a lake. Upon our arrival, a terrified and crying teenage fireman ran carrying the child to me. As the child was laid in my arms, I noticed in the headlights of the ambulance her blue lips and eyes wide open with a slight glaze over them. All the way to Kennestone Hospital, about a twenty-minute ride with full lights and siren, I worked frantically to revive her.

On the way to the emergency room, I managed to get her heart started, but I wasn't able to get her breathing again. Quickly, I donned my headset and punched the hospital frequency.

"Cherokee to Kennestone ER. Priority call." As I waited for a response from the emergency room, I gave her mouth-to-mouth.

"This is Kennestone. Go ahead Cherokee."

I didn't hear the response. I was focused so intently on the child that my driver had to flick the compartment lights on and off to get my attention.

"Catfish! Hospital callin ya!"

I pressed the microphone, "Kennestone. Coming straight at you with a two-year-old female. Possible drowning. ETA is 10 to 15 minutes. No breath sounds. Heart rate estimated at more than 120. Eyes fully dilated. Full rebreather. Ambubag. Need manpower on arrival. Requesting no orders at this time. Cherokee out!"

They responded, "Received Cherokee. We'll be waiting. Cherokee? Can you start an IV?"

I had already taken off my headset and had started to work on the little girl. My driver again flicked the lights off and on to get my attention.

"Yeah?"

"They want to know . . . can you start an IeeeVeee?"

I was reaching up to the top compartment to retrieve the Ambubag. "No. Tell them to get a team for a cutdown." The little girl's veins had all but disappeared, and she would require minor surgery to insert a tube directly into a vein.

I knew if I didn't get her breathing now, her heart would stop and we would be back to square one. It would be harder the second time around. Her eyes opened and her mouth gaped wide open, desperately trying to breathe. The forced compressed oxygen was not getting into her lungs. As a last resort, which was totally out of line, I flipped her over on her side and compressed her stomach several times. I was counting on getting her to vomit the pizza that I was sure was keeping her from breathing. Her throat appeared clear with no abnormalities. When that didn't work, I picked her up and laid her across both my knees, and then I slapped her on the back repeatedly. Again nothing happened. I tried mouth-to-mouth resuscitation, forcing my breath into her lungs. Nothing. Her eyes started to close and her heartbeat began to slow down with alarming speed. Her skin began to turn a light blue.

I flipped her on her side, across my knee, and decided to hell with it! I inserted two fingers into the back of her throat, compressing her tongue at the same time to keep her from swallowing it, to provoke her to vomit. It worked! A stream of vomitus, consisting of largely undigested pepperoni, spewed forth and she was able to breath again. My God! I must've lost ten years of my life when I snatched her back from the grasp of the Grim Reaper. A child leaves a much more lasting impression on a firefighter or an EMT than does an adult.

5

Midnight on the Graveyard Shift

One of the more dramatic episodes of my career began when the dispatcher at Fulton County 911 in downtown Atlanta advised my unit that Atlanta Fire Rescue One was on the scene of a premature infant call, and requested our ETA. I had just been listed involuntarily on the midnight roster as the technician assigned on a basic unit to Zone 504, in the southwest corner of the city. We called that area the Combat Zone, as it was known for gunshot calls and gang warfare.

I was particularly familiar with the Crips, since it was their territory that we patrolled in between emergency calls. They had a fearsome and bad-ass reputation for leaving a nasty calling card whenever they killed a target. Automatic gunfire would rip huge chunks of muscle, bone, and tissue from the legs of the victim, just to keep them from running any further. The leader of the gang would then perform the coup de grace with a .25-caliber to the back of the head. They let us know that they did not appreciate intrusion on their turf from any outsiders, as a bystander once advised me as we stood and looked at another dead gang victim lying up against a brick wall. The twelve-year-old boy had tried to "steal" customers away from the gang and had paid for it with his life. I knew a cop who kept a small notebook with a listing of the various calling cards left by the different gangs. I often tugged at my bulletproof vest, wondering if it could even begin to stop a bullet.

Holding up five long bony fingers, my partner indicated that we were five minutes away from the infant call. I got on the radio: "504 to Radio. Advise ETA is five out. Can you advise?"

The ambulance backfired loudly. The echo reverberated inside the metal cab of the truck and died before the vehicle coasted to a stop in the middle of a street littered with rotting garbage, broken wine bottles, and dead rats. A bad place to break down.

I got on the radio again. "504 to Radio! Advise Code 95. Unit 504 is 32 at MLK and J. P. Brawley. Request 91 for 81. Provide ETA and notify 415 of 504's status as 10–7."

A wino, hanging with all his might on to a scarred, stapled light pole, jerked suddenly at the sound of the backfire to fall face-first onto the piss-stained sidewalk. We looked over to watch him slide quickly into a classic grand mal seizure of proportions not previously recorded in medical journals. Foam, saliva, and spit sprayed everywhere. Sweat had mingled with the dust of his woolen clothes while lice, big as south Georgia gnats, attacked the exposed and grimy skin. His legs and arms seemed to be attached to a nuclear reactor. A message came crackling over the radio: "Received, 504. EMS copy 95. Out of service. Be advised all units currently on call. None available for backup."

I told the dispatcher to stand by. "Hey, look what you've done now," I said to my partner, indicating the distressed wino. My partner just shrugged his shoulders and told me to lock my doors.

I got back on the radio—at least the battery still

worked—"504 to Radio. Stand by while I try to contact Rescue One on our call." She acknowledged us briefly.

Turning to my partner, I poked him in the ribs with my microphone and pointed over to the wino. "Ya better go on over there and . . ."

He reached behind him and retrieved a backpack. "Hell, no!" he said. "You're the tech. You go. I ain't gettin' out of the truck. Not here!"

My partner tried to start the truck, to no avail, and decided to take a quick inventory of his backpack. He pulled a switchblade out of the pack and released the safety. The long thin blade snapped with a sharp click. He unlocked the door, got out, and walked to the front of the truck. I watched my partner open the hood, look into the engine compartment, and shake his head slowly after waving away some of the steam emitting from the radiator. He proclaimed it dead, Catholic-style, gently closed the hood, and got back inside. We didn't need to attract the attention of the addicts who, we knew, were lurking in the dark.

After locking his side of the door and placing the switchblade on his thigh, he leaned over slowly toward me. I gave him a funny look and said, in my best imitation of a southern belle, "You ain't gonna kiss me, are you, honey?"

He ignored me and motioned with a gentle nod of his head. "There's a couple of 'em hidin' in those bushes over there. See 'em?" He pointed a single finger through the windshield toward some high hedges on the other side of the street. "Jesus!" I said, "and we ain't got no firepower. Do ya think we oughta call in an air strike and have the flypukes throw a couple of napalms?"

When I saw several more dark figures moving about, it became serious. "Yeah! I see 'em, too. Ain't too cool here."

I reached down to feel the ankle holster containing my

.25-caliber automatic, just to reassure myself that it hadn't fallen out again. "Ain't much we can do here," I said. "Sit tight and wait for backup, or else get ambushed. We're sitting ducks here. Did you have to pick this neighborhood? If we start walkin' . . ."

"Get our asses shot," my partner interjected. He reached for his backpack again and started to rummage through it.

"One of these days somebody's gonna take it away from you and kill your black ass," I said. He decided to hold on to the switchblade.

"Give me your radio," I said. "Mine is dead already."

He unclipped his radio from his belt and handed it to me before he went back to eyeballing our immediate perimeter for possible threats. "Oh yeah," I said, "if any of them come near this truck, turn on all the lights and hit the siren box. That oughta throw one or two of 'em into a fit and maybe you can handle the rest of them, Rambo."

He began fiddling with the console buttons, making sure all of the switches were in the "On" position and that the master switch was off. That way he could activate all the lights and sirens at the same time, with one flip of the master switch. It was a wonderful way to ward off unwelcome guests.

I keyed the microphone and called our dispatcher to ask if any other trucks had gone back into service yet. She replied negatively. I sat up straight and readjusted my bulletproof vest. I was starting to worry. "504 to Radio? Is there a truck out with Rescue One yet?"

She meekly answered, "No, 504."

"Have you contacted 415?"

"No response on landline or radio."

"Have you contacted 416, 417, or 418?"

"No response."

I had assumed that the supervisor could handle this call. "Where the hell could he be?" I asked my partner.

"Probably havin' a heart attack," was his response.

Number 415 was the supervisor for the morning watch, from 10 p.m. until 7 a.m., and he was an old, long-ago "burned-out" EMT who was having a heart attack every other week. He refused so many treatments that the EMTs would simply keep walking if they saw him having chest pains in his squad car.

There was nothing I could do at this point but wait for another unit to come back into service and respond. I asked my partner to try starting the truck again.

Again, nothing happened.

I decided it was time for another injection of morbid humor. I turned to my partner and matter-of-factly asked, "Hey, what do you give a dead baby?"

"What?" He was taken aback.

"What do you give a dead baby?" I asked again.

"A funeral?" he ventured.

"No, a dead puppy," I said with a laugh.

"Mannnnn! You are one sick deaf and dumb muther!"

All of a sudden, I was mad as hell. I threw the mike down on the floorboard, turned, and grabbed him by the collar to pull him closer to me. At the same time, I laid my hand on his switchblade. "If you ever so much as call me deaf and dumb one more time, I'm going to beat your black ass and rip your balls off!" I had been listening to these degrading references for too long. The other EMTs would freely use the expression "deaf and dumb" to me and anyone else, for that matter. I had begun to take it a little more personally every day.

After this outburst, my partner calmly asked, "Is your door locked, Catfish?"

I let go of him, picked up my mike, and turned my hearing aid up a bit more. The battery was starting to die, which forced me to turn the volume to the point just before it starts to feedback.

All of a sudden a face slammed into the driver's side window, with the nose pressed at a crazy angle and bleeding, then disappeared as if it had never been there to start with. My partner screamed, punched the master switch, and jumped into my lap while pointing the tip of the switchblade toward the offending window. There was still some blood smeared on the glass. "Ooooooooooohhhh shittt, Momma! Turn on the lights!" The ambulance immediately came to life with all the flood lamps, horns blaring, strobes flashing, and siren on yelp mode. I began stabbing the emergency button on my dead portable radio and reaching for my pistol, which slipped from my sweaty grasp to fall into the wheel well. I was more concerned with not hearing the tone emitting from the portable, signifying that a Grady unit was in serious trouble. I kept stabbing the emergency button on the radio before I realized that the battery was dead. At the same time that I was reaching for my partner's portable radio, my right leg and foot were searching for the pistol. I quickly thought better of that activity, for fear that the gun would go off and shoot a hole in my foot. Without taking the radio from my partner's hand, I punched the bright red button. The main radio on the floorboard and the portable radio suddenly erupted into a long loud deep tone, followed by "Fulton County to all units. Cease traffic until further notice. Grady 504? Do you wish to declare an emergency?"

Now I couldn't think of a damn thing to say. My partner turned off the master switch, and when he did, the cab light began to dim. "Oh shit!" he said. "The battery is goin' dead. It's on eight now." Fourteen was considered a full charge. The full load had sucked the juice from the battery and there was just enough left to operate the main radio. "Keep the radio on 1, and I'll keep the portable on 2."

We looked out our rearview mirrors and decided that the lights and sirens had done the trick. I was just surprised not to see a body or two around the truck having a seizure. "I guess we're okay now," I said.

He nodded and settled back into his seat. "Fulton County to Grady 504? Advise status."

I picked up the radio. "504 to Radio. Disregard." I was in no mood to explain.

"Received. All Grady units resume traffic. Acknowledged by unit numbers. Time out at 0205 hours."

I tried contacting Rescue One again. "Grady Five-zero-four to Atlanta Fire Rescue One. How do you copy?" I was getting quite frustrated. It had only been ten minutes since we broke down, and already it was starting to look like another bad day at work. I took the mike from my partner and called the dispatcher.

"504 Radio. Have you got 415 on landline yet?"

"Negative." She got smart and decided to put the monkey on my back. "504, how do you advise?"

"Radio," I said, "do you have a private on rotation?"

"That's affirmative, 504. Atlanta South is next. Do you wish for me to contact them and get them started for your location?"

I tried to imagine that I was in the front office having to deal with this one. I saw no option other than getting a private ambulance to respond to a Grady call. Only the front office had the authority to grant requests for 911 to use a private ambulance service. So far, I had created grounds to have myself suspended without pay or dismissed outright for authorizing the dispatcher to use a private ambulance service. "Radio, reroute the private to our location after a Grady unit 10-8. Atlanta South may have the seizure patient at our location."

The driver asked me if that was legitimate for the dispatcher to reroute Atlanta South. He could understand getting a private en route against regulations, but to reroute it? "Mannnnnn," I said, "there ain't nothin' legit tonight! Where the hell is 415?"

The dispatcher called back and said that Atlanta South gave a fifteen-minute ETA.

"Radio," I said, "Where are they responding from?"

"They advised from their station."

I turned to my partner and asked, "Where is that?"

"In East Point. Just south of it by the hospital."

That's too far away, I thought.

"Radio, can we use another private, closer to the call?"

"Negative. Protocol specifies order of the rotation list."

I could understand that. Most of the privates dotting the city, mostly on the south side, applied to the county for a spot on the rotation list. This was to ensure fair treatment and that an equal amount of emergency and nonemergency calls were handled by the various services. The list was used on the authority of the EMS supervisor if there were no other Grady trucks available and only after a certain amount of time had elapsed for a call holding. If a Grady truck was not in service after a call had been holding for so many minutes, then the call was automatically given to the next private ambulance service on the list.

I looked at my watch again. It had been more than fifteen minutes. I called the medics at the scene once more. The channel exploded with screaming, hollering, and loud talking in the background. "Need a truck down here nowwww!" someone shouted. "Can't get it breathin'. Can anybody hear us, for God's sake?"

I damn near jumped out of my seat. I immediately stabbed another key on the microphone. "Grady Five-zero-four to Rescue One. How do you copy, Rescue One? Advise status!" I got nothing but more static.

"Grady 504 to Rescue One, dammit, you are in a dead spot. Move the radio around! Advise status."

I tried once more. "Grady 504 to Rescue One. Advise now or make a landline. If you copy me, advise Code 95. Code 95. No go. Hang in there. Will come for you."

I turned the portable radio on and called EMS. "504 Radio! On one."

At least they answered. "Received, 504. No contact with 415. ETA is still fifteen."

My hand holding the mike fell to my lap. I waited a moment to absorb that last piece of information. "Radio to 504. Copy my last?" I clicked twice in acknowledgment.

"Atlanta Fire Dispatch to Grady 504." I quickly brought my mike up to my lips.

"504. Go ahead, Fire."

"Advise I have APD dispatched to Rescue One's location for priority welfare check. . . ." The channel that we were talking on exploded into more screaming arguments, and just as suddenly stopped broadcasting. I had the impression that the medics were looking for a better reception area to receive and transmit on their portable radio. The radio waves on all of the communication equipment worked on a direct line of sight.

"504 to Fire. Raise them on another tac and advise them of our status. Code 95. Atlanta South is en route to their location. ETA is fifteen."

Before the Atlanta Fire Dispatch could respond, I heard,

"Rescue One to Grady . . . four." They were fading in and out.

I jumped in and spoke quickly, "504 to Rescue One. No go. No go. Private fifteen ETA. Advise status."

Miraculously, he answered. "Premature infant bor . . . toil . . . CPR in . . . gress."

I turned to my partner, who said, "I think they got a preemie in full arrest. CPR in progress, and something about a toilet."

I keyed the microphone again. "Okay, Rescue One. Continue CPR. Private en route. Any minute now. Stand by."

I switched over to EMS and asked for a new ETA on Atlanta South's response. "Uh, 504? They gave me another fifteen minutes ETA."

In frustration I kicked the firewall under the dashboard and threw the clipboard in the back of the truck. I didn't know what else to do except switch back to the medics. "Oh God! We need a truck now!"

That did it. I switched back to the EMS dispatcher and said that I had no choice but to run to the call. It was only eight blocks away. My driver jumped and said, "You're gonna what?"

I got out of the truck and started to gather my jumpkit, my metal flashlight, and the portable radio with the good battery. I pulled the automatic from the ankle holster and put it in my back pocket for easy access.

"You're gonna what, now?" The driver leaned all the way over again while tapping me on the shoulder.

I just looked up and said, "Huh?"

"Don't give me that shit. You heard me! Why are you going to risk getting your white ass shot off?"

"I haven't got a choice, man! Do you have a suggestion?"

He leaned back into his seat. "Hell no! If I was you,

which I ain't, I wouldn't go. Ain't nothin' can be done for them. They're on their own."

"Well, you can kiss my ass. I have to go."

To reassure myself that the dispatcher understood my intention I called her again. "504 technician to Radio. Copy my last transmission?"

She replied meekly that she did.

"Also, Radio, my partner will remain with the truck. Try to drag APD from Krispy Kreme and get them down here. We still need another truck for the seizure patient." I looked over through the open door and could still see lying on the ground, the wino deep in a drunken slumber, curled up in a fetal position.

"Advise fire dispatcher to relay that I should be at Rescue One's location in about five minutes."

"Received, 504 technician. Please use extreme caution and advise me ASAP upon your arrival. Time out at 0218 hours."

While readjusting the strap around my shoulder and turning the portable radio on, I told my partner to keep trying to reach the medics to let them know that I was coming on foot.

At that point I realized that my hearing aid had finally gone dead. I took it out and put it carefully in my pocket. I decided not to bother changing the battery. I wasn't planning to stop and have a conversation with anybody in that neighborhood.

At first I tried to stick to the shadows, but that proved to be dangerous and foolish. I was forced to run down the middle of the street, which was weakly illuminated by bullet-pocked street lights. When I arrived, huffing and puffing, there was a lone fire rescue truck in front of a dilapidated old apartment building that had been condemned by the city. I walked as carefully as I could to avoid stepping into the piss-filled potholes of what had once been a sidewalk. A cop came out of the building and saw me. He hollered out, "Hey, I was just comin' to get ya." He stood on the front landing, looking down at me. "How did ya get here?" I could see he was looking for my ambulance.

I took a deep breath and looked back toward where I had come from. "I ran all the way here. 'Bout eight blocks." The cop stood there dumbfounded.

"You ran all the way here?" he asked. "What's your name, so I can tell the guys back at the Krispy Kreme?"

"You can call me Catfish," I said.

Taking out my portable, I called the dispatcher. "504 Tech to Radio. 10-7 with Rescue One. Code 4." I could almost hear the EMS dispatcher breathe a sigh of relief.

"Received. I copy you 10-7 with Rescue One at 0227 hours. Advise ASAP. Atlanta South still en route."

I stepped through the doorway and walked carefully down the dark hallway. The floor was slippery, and the powerful aroma of old urine shimmered against the lonely light bulb that hung forlornly at the end of the hallway. At the very end was a knot of people gathered at the door of an apartment. One of the winos had stepped back and turned to puke a stream of vomitus against the hallway wall. He wiped his mouth with the sleeve of his tattered shirt and resumed watching in a drunken stupor.

I took a breath and made my way down the hall. The aroma was overwhelming. I had to stop to dry-puke before I could make my announcement. "Grady here!"

As if caught by surprise, the small crowd stiffened with fear and parted like the Red Sea. I stopped dead in my tracks and watched with utter disgust. I could just barely see into the hell hole they called a bathroom. The tub was filled with rotting garbage, and the stench was unbearable. I quickly tore off the filters from two cigarettes and stuck them in my nostrils.

A black woman was sitting on a cracked, leaking toilet stolen from another abandoned apartment and set over a sewage hole in the floor. She was semiconscious and leaning her wet hair against the sweaty chest of a man who was standing next to her.

The medics were working frantically inside a small shoebox placed right up against the toilet, as far as the newborn baby's umbilical cord could reach. "Hey! I'm here!" My voice echoed softly in the close confines of the bathroom. They both looked back over their shoulders, and their desperation was forgotten. One medic was compressing tenderly, with perfect rhythm, with one index finger on the almost transparent chest of the premature infant. The other medic was holding an oxygen tube near the incredibly tiny nostrils. "Y'all are doing fine," I said. "Keep it up. I'll call Radio and get us another ETA on Atlanta South. They should already be here."

They simply grunted an approval. I reached for my portable radio, only to find it dead. I immediately reached over and took the shoulder mike from one of the medics and called their dispatcher. "Grady 504 Tech to Atlanta Fire. Advise radio is dead. Relay to EMS. Top priority clearance. Requesting a 4 here now!"

"Received, 504 Tech. Stand by."

I reclipped the mike to the medic's strap and reached for my jumpkit. "Just keep doin' what you're doin'. You're doin' great. I'm gonna go ahead and cut the cord." I patted one of the medics on the back to reassure him. He simply grunted. I used to have a partner who wondered if that was the extent of the typical medic's vocabulary.

Sweat, blood, and tears rolled off our faces as we tried to prolong the life of the baby. I recalled that we actually did not give a shit about the woman on the toilet. She had injected "Mexican mud" and said she had to take a shit. Instead, she had shit a baby and damn near overdosed on the toilet before someone called 911.

I can't help but wonder whether this incident helped change my feelings about the issue of abortion. I think it's real sad that a living child has to be born this way.

While tearing open the OB kit, I asked the medics what had happened. I was searching for a pair of sterile gloves when the medics related, ". . . found the bitch taking a shit with a needle in her arm. Asshole here . . . ," he said, pointing to the man holding the woman's head up, "said he's the father and they never knew she was pregnant. She even shit on the kid, too!"

The baby was pulled out of the cramped space, wrapped in a large trauma dressing, and placed in a shoebox. I took the umbilical cord and tugged on it gently to check for tension against the afterbirth, or placenta, and I realized that it wouldn't be ready for at least another twenty minutes. "Have you got a pulse?" I asked.

I retrieved two hemostats and clamped them on the umbilical cord, about eight inches apart. "No! That why I'm doin' C, P, and R. Of course I don't have a pulse."

"No, I meant stop and check the brachial for a pulse." Looking into the jumpkit, I located the scalpel and prepared to cut the cord.

"Nothing," the medic said. He resumed CPR after checking the brachial artery for a pulse. Two sections of the cord had been tied off with hemostats, permitting me to cut in between. I kept one end of both severed sections of the cord pointed away so that residual, blood, and fluid would spurt against the side of the tub. A large German cockroach scampered away to avoid the splash.

"Okay," I said. "You can back away from the toilet and take the box outa here."

One of the winos, watching from the doorway of the apartment, had to ask. There's one in every crowd. "Hey mon, why you talk like you got shit in your mouth?"

The fire medics' radio had just announced that Atlanta South gave a five-minute ETA. I tried to ignore the wino's question. He asked again, this time more boldly. "Hey! Me talkin' to you. Why mon talk like he got shit in his mouth?" He put his hand on my shoulder, and I instantly recoiled and took out my metal maglight and held it like a baseball bat. The wino laughed and turned to slap his buddy on the back. His buddy, not expecting the friendly slap on the back, spit out his mouthful of cheap-ass wine. The buddy reeled back and coldcocked the laughing wino. He turned back and begged for another mouthful.

"Goddammit!" I shouted. "I want everybody outa here. Now!"

Nobody moved a muscle. They continued to stare with reddened sightless eyes until I said, "Okay, fine. Radio, get me about four Grady trucks here. I got some winos and assholes to take to the detox center. Advise them that we are going to need to dry them out." I keyed the dead portable radio. They all climbed over each other in their haste to leave the building. Several made comments on their way out. "Them Grady ride with the devils!" and "Not me, not Grady, no sir! Never come out alive." Yeah, well, I thought, there are plenty of people who would give anything to come down to Grady for a bite to eat and a chance for a bed to sleep in for the night.

I threw one of the medics a sterile prepackaged suction.

"Get that kid suctioned out." I pointed to the other medic and asked, "Get the mother out on the bed and raise her legs. She goes out on the next bus. As soon as a truck gets here, you and I will go with the kid, and you stay with the mother." I used their radio again and called their dispatcher. I wanted to know whether he could get me another ETA on Atlanta South and find out whether any Grady trucks had gone back into service. "Stand-by One."

While waiting in the middle of the scene that unfolded around me, I tried to remain calm in spite of the situation. As much as I tried to avoid playing God, the decisions that I made would determine whether the premature infant would live or die. I could feel the tip of the Grim Reaper's blade trailing softly down the back of my neck, just sharp enough to let me know. I was shaken awake, from a bad dream to a real nightmare, when the medic, who was still doing compression on the infant, asked, "What now, Catfish?"

It took me a moment before I said, "I won't fuck with you guys, but nothin' now." They both grunted and kept on working.

The fire dispatcher called back to advise that no trucks were available and that Atlanta South still gave an ETA of five minutes. "Radio," I said, "are they lost or what? I need a truck here now." An idea popped into my head. "Radio, get me that cop who was just here at our location. Get him back here for a Code 1 run to Grady. Now!"

I turned to the second medic and said, "Stay with her and turn her head to the side if she vomits. Atlanta South will be here any minute. You ride in with them. We'll see you back at Grady, and I'll buy you a Coke."

I knew that what I was considering would break every rule and regulation in the state health laws and protocols mandated by Grady Hospital, but if a ride to the hospital in a police car could buy me the time I needed to save the infant, so be it.

"Fire dispatch to Grady 504 Tech!"

"Yeah, go ahead!"

"APD gave one-minute ETA and has been advised. Good luck!"

Great. Fantastic. I wanted this to be over now. While we all waited and waited, I kept looking at my watch. The tension was gnawing at my stomach, and I could feel the whole humid night sky starting to push down on me. My heart was pounding like wild mustangs running hell-bent for freedom.

"Where the hell is he?" I wondered. I could hear a siren growing from a faint wail to a loud yelp before being shut off a few blocks away. I could see the powerful strobes flashing through the dark trees and bouncing off of buildings, but they were red and white, not blue. Strange! I started to reach for the mike on the medic's shoulder when Atlanta South pulled up to a dusty stop right in front of us.

The side doors of the fancy rig popped open and a rather large female EMT presented herself with open arms waiting to take the shoebox from us. Just as we started to hand it to her, a Grady ambulance miraculously appeared, along with a supervisor's car, right behind Atlanta South. "Whoaa! We'll take it from here. You can go right in and take the mother to Grady." The EMT was relieved to know there was still a paying customer.

At the hospital, the five-months-premature infant died after our arrival. The physician on call in the ER waltzed into the treatment room and simply pronounced the infant dead. He turned to the medic and said, "You can stop now!" and left. The medic continued to perform CPR but started to slack off after a few more minutes. He finally stopped altogether and laid his head down on the treatment bench. I knew he wanted to be left alone, and I quietly left for my own corner. I found a place deep inside the bowels of the hospital, under the basement, and I sat down and cried.

I had left my partner to fend for himself, run through the worst neighborhood in the state, worked the infant call, gotten no help from our supervisor, and then maintained life support on the way to the hospital. We had sweat blood and tears on what was medically termed a fetus with undeveloped gender. I later found out that the son of a bitch who claimed to be the husband was in fact the brother of the woman and the father of the dead fetus. It wasn't until this writing that I suddenly and shamefully realized that we could have used the medics' truck parked outside the whole damn time.

6

The Bleeding House

A few years ago there was much talk about the house that oozed blood on the west side of Atlanta. I was one of a handful of people who knew the real story. The elderly couple claimed that a ghost resided in their house. It became one of many ghost stories that haunted the city.

It was nearly 3 a.m. when the assistant supervisor, Ray, approached me in the hallway of Grady Hospital to ask me a favor.

"Sure, what's up?" My partner and I had just dropped off a patient for treatment of the worst case of venereal disease that I have ever seen, or smelled for, that matter. She was a grandmother, times eight, at age thirty-eight, when she called us for a ride to Grady. She was leaking fluid from the affected area, and the stench forced my driver to drive with his head out the window. He couldn't take it much longer, and turned the call into a quiet Code 2 with just lights. I kept stuffing nonsterile gauze over my nose and mouth while holding my breath.

"Where's your partner?" Ray asked. He stood tall, more than six feet, and had moved up to assistant supervisor in a short period of time. Some have it and some don't. Ray was a man who had the little people's respect.

"I think he's already out in the truck, probably asleep at the wheel."

"Go get him. I need to talk to you both in my office. Don't go into service and stay off the radio until I tell you."

This took me by complete surprise. I searched my memory for any recent complaints that could have been filed against me. Nothing. I couldn't remember punching out a patient lately.

"Ray, are we in trouble again?" I asked, bored. It wasn't uncommon to get slapped with a piece of paper notifying me of so many days off with or without pay, usually without a reason.

As it turned out, I wasn't in trouble. Ray had gotten a bizarre report and wanted us to check it out. The location of the strange call was but a few miles from the hospital, and we arrived well within the ten-minute time limit imposed by the higher-ups. Most of us tended to stop and get a bite to eat or run an errand on the way to a Code 3, meaning there was no hurry.

As we turned left from Martin Luther King Drive, we spotted a black man waiting by a mailbox. In the bright glare of our headlights, my partner turned his spotlight on. We studied the immediate area for any potential ambush points before we were satisfied that it was secure. As soon as I pulled the truck to a stop, alongside the mailbox, I turned on all of the lamps to illuminate the scene until we were sure what we were getting into. The black man stepped up to my window and reached into his breast pocket.

"Hold it! Hold it!" I said. "Keep your hands where I can see them! And step away from the truck."

This was another rule for survival on the streets. Always watch a person's hands, and especially their eyes. Maintaining eye contact with a patient allowed me to maintain control, in most cases.

The man refused to comply with my request, and my foot became a little heavier as I prepared to drive off immediately, in case he pulled out a gun. Instead, he pulled out a badge and identified himself as a homicide detective with the Atlanta Police Department. I turned off all the lights on the truck and dimmed the headlights, as well. There was no need to call more attention to ourselves.

"Yeah?" I said, looking at his identification. "I'm Catfish, and this here is my partner."

"I appreciate you guys comin' down to help me."

I put the truck in park and we began to climb out. "So what can we do for you? Our assistant supervisor, Ray, sent us down here on some kind of a favor."

"That's right," he said. "Ray and I go back a long way. I asked him to send somebody down here to tell me if what I found is blood."

My partner, John Athens, a thin bearded EMT, asked with concern, "Blood?"

"Yeah, I think it's blood. I just need somebody to check it out and tell me if it's human blood."

John asked with even more concern, "Is there a body inside?"

"Oh no! No bodies inside. Just my parents. Anyway, come on inside and tell me if it's human blood. Okay? I'll take care of the rest. I'm sure Ray told y'all to keep a lid on this?"

"Uh, yeah, sir, he did."

John and I looked at each other. We shrugged our shoulders again and followed him to the front door. It was heavily barred with metal, as was the rest of the house.

"Are your parents . . . alive?"

"Of course," he said. "Just come on in and I'll tell you what's happening."

I wasn't so sure about this. I was ready to just stop and say forget it and go back to Ray and ask him to send someone else out here. I was in no mood to go looking for trouble.

As soon as the police officer unlocked the second door and opened it, we were completely stunned by the powerfully sweet aroma of blood that saturated the entire living room. The carpet was soaked with what appeared to be blood. My first impression was that a large animal had been brutally butchered and its blood collected and spread evenly on the carpet. Upon closer examination I noticed that blood had already begun to stain the walls as it progressed upward from the baseboards. In the far corner of the living room sat an elderly couple, fully dressed and appearing very calm despite the presence of the blood.

Goosebumps, chills, sweats, and fear gripped me as I stood at the front door of the living room of hell.

John had already taken out a blood vial used for drawing blood via an IV stick and taken a sample from the carpet.

"So do you think it's human?" the detective asked.

"Could be. Could be an animal," John said. He looked over at the policeman's parents on the couch. "Are they okay? Do you want me to check them over?"

"Fine, go ahead."

Meanwhile, I decided to take a tour of the rest of the house. The detective walked back to the front door and locked both the metal gate and the door.

"Wait," I said. "If you don't mind, please leave the door open." I had a terrible phobia about being locked in a stranger's house, or any house, for that matter. I wanted to be able to escape in a hurry, with nothing in my way.

"Okay if I take a look around?" I asked the detective.

He simply nodded and said, "Sure."

"Sir, what happened here?" I asked.

He stood up, adjusted his belt and sighed.

"I mean, if you want us to help you, then you help us."

He agreed and motioned for me to come into the kitchen. "Mother was in the shower when she noticed blood coming through the drain, then it came through the shower nozzle. When she got out of the shower, she said that the toilet was vomiting blood all over the floor."

I was convinced that this house was haunted. There's no way one body could bleed that much. I had a flashback to my own ghost story that occurred after my marriage to my childhood sweetheart, Gina, when we had moved into a new apartment in downtown Indianapolis. I never have figured out what that was about.

The policeman went on with his story. "So she stepped into the hallway and started to freak out when she saw all the blood. She said she saw footprints on the carpet leading into their bedroom. She thought my father had been killed, but he was just asleep until she woke him up. He looked down from the bed and saw all the blood. They called me and I got here as fast as I could."

None of this seemed right. First of all, why weren't the cops crawling all over the place with forensic people, considering the amount of blood found. Second, why was the old couple so calm about all this? I'd expect most people to go to pieces. Third, why weren't they outside instead of calmly sitting on the couch with blood everywhere. Fourth, why had the detective locked his own parents inside the house? And then I wondered what kind of a favor Ray owed this detective. There was certainly nothing in it for me and John.

The policeman went on to explain, "My father is on dialysis, down at the clinic, I don't know where. He stays in bed a lot, and when my mother called me, I thought maybe a line got pulled out accidentally, but when I got here . . ."

I followed him down the hallway, keeping my hands to my side to avoid touching or brushing against the walls. Blood was everywhere. The smell did not offend me as much as the sheer quantity of it. I had never been one to faint or feel queasy at the sight of it. We passed the bathroom and indeed, there was blood in the stopped-up toilet. The shower stall was dark red and dripped to the red floor from the towel handles. It was incredible.

When we walked into the bedroom, I noticed several sets of footprints overlapping each other. There was blood everywhere in the bedroom as well. There were several pieces of medical equipment used for dialysis patients positioned alongside the bed. "Could my father have bled this much?" he asked.

"No, I'm afraid not," I said. "If he had, he'd be dead for sure. If you asked me again, I'd say blood in this quantity would have to have come from more than ten bodies."

The detective nodded in agreement. "I have never in my career seen this much."

There was something funny going on and I wanted no part of it. My partner, John, met me in the kitchen while the detective huddled with his parents in a private conversation.

I told John that the old man was a dialysis patient.

"Oh?" he said. "He didn't tell me that. Neither one of them wanted to talk to me much anyhow. What's going on?"

"Beats me. Let's get outa here as soon as you check the old man."

John pulled out his gear from different pockets and took his stethoscope from around his neck.

"Let me know when you're ready to go, " I said. "I'll hold on to your portable."

"What portable?"

"What do you mean, what portable? The radio, man! Did you leave it in the truck? You carry all that shit and you didn't bring the radio?"

I was getting irritated.

"Naw, man," he said. "I though you had it."

"How long have you ridden with me? I'm deaf and dumb according to you, remember?"

He just shrugged his shoulders and walked back to the living room to begin a workup on the old man. He almost slipped on the blood.

John found nothing wrong with the man, and we realized that there was nothing more we could do.

After we got back to the hospital, Ray was waiting in his office for a report. John acted as if he were headed for the bathroom, when he was actually going to the lab on the fourth floor. A buddy of his had said he would be able to get a fix on the blood sample. Meanwhile, Ray was giving me further instructions about keeping quiet or else losing our jobs.

"Is that all, sir?" I asked.

"Yes," he said. "Get back to work."

When I saw John again, I asked him, "So, what did you find out?"

"It came from a blood bank over on Piedmont."

"No shit! How'd they find out?"

"All blood banks leave some sort of a marker in the sample to identify the source of the donation, or something like that . . ."

"I still don't understand this."

A few days later, I asked Ray what the hell was going on with this case. Ray had apparently had a change of attitude about the whole situation and seemed to distance himself from his friend the detective when he found out a few things on his own. He told me later, "The detective's mother went down to the clinic with her husband and stole bags of blood from the bank, took them home, and 'painted' the whole house while her husband was asleep." I was amazed.

When the book about Atlanta ghosts came out, this story appeared as one of the chapters. Apparently the old couple had decided to capitalize on the story, thinking there was nobody to dispute it. I hope the detective had resigned or gone somewhere else by time the book came out.

7

Amazing Grace

*T*he city of Atlanta was quiet, almost too quiet for comfort. It was the last week of the month, and people were sitting on a razor's edge after running out of money for drugs and alcohol. It wouldn't take much to set them off, and thank God the weather had finally grown cooler after a summer-long heat wave. With no calls holding, all of the trucks were at their stations in different parts of the city to wait for the next call. My unit, Grady Unit 302 Morning, was parked in front of Atlanta Fire Station 10 on Moreland Avenue at Interstate 20. My partner had already fallen asleep in the back while I stayed in the cab to finish up some paperwork that had to be turned in at the end of the shift.

The radio crackled with static as the dispatcher called our unit. "302 Mornin'. Out at 10." I reached over to get a pen and the driver's log sheet in preparation for taking down the information needed to respond to the call.

"Received 302. Make Landline to EMS for information. Time out at 0230."

This meant she wanted me to call her on the phone, and when I did, she asked me if I would do her a favor. "So," I said, "you want us to go to Burger King?" I took out my pen and tore a scrap of paper from a stack of newspapers.

"Not a bad idea," she replied, "but that's not it. I need you to go over and see this lady."

"What is it? A sick call?" I asked. I was still poised with my pen ready to copy something down. It was much easier for me to get information over the phone than through the radio. Fortunately, the fire station was dark and quiet. All of the firemen had gone to bed, making it easier for me to hear.

"No, the woman said that there was nothing wrong with her. She has called about four or five times in the last hour, though."

"Well, what's wrong, then?" I asked.

"I guess she wants to talk to somebody. She sounds like a real nice lady. She said that she lives by herself and doesn't have anyone to talk to. I couldn't help but think of you. I was sure you would go over and talk to her."

I had a better idea. "What's wrong with the cops? Can't they go over and say hello?" I was dying to grab forty winks, but I didn't. I owed this dispatcher so many favors that I had to oblige her every chance I got.

"We were going to call them, but we thought you could do the job better. You're so sweet, and you listen to people."

That did it. She had me again with that sexy voice of hers. I switched my hearing aid from the telephone mode to the off position. I didn't need it since things were so quiet at the station. "Go ahead and give me the address, and I'll be on my way."

After the information was copied down on the driver's log sheet, I realized that the call was in another zone. "Hey," I asked, "where's 505? This is out of our zone. How do you advise?" She waited a moment, obviously checking with her superiors.

"That's right, Catfish. They're picking up a body at Grady for transport to the morgue."

OK, I thought, better them than us. I'll be happy to take this other call. "OK, we're gone. Will call out when we get there. Bye."

As I walked out to the ambulance parked and ready to go on the driveway, I had a nagging feeling that something was about to happen. I decided to let my partner sleep through the call while I handled this lady who kept calling just to talk to someone. I opened the back doors of the ambulance and the lights came on automatically. I explained to my partner what the deal was, and he went back to sleep after pulling a blanket from one of the compartments.

I didn't have any trouble at all locating the apartment when I pulled into the compound of the worst housing project in North America. To the left I spotted an open door with a light on in the kitchen. An old woman stood waiting with her hands to her sides, just inside the doorway. After parking the truck for easy egress, if need be, I called the EMS dispatcher and radioed, "302 out." She answered with a time. The lady gently waved at me and motioned for me to come inside, which I did after locking the truck with an extra set of keys. I like to keep my motor running when I'm on a call. "Uh, . . . hi there! Grady EMS. How can I help you?"

She was wearing an old housecoat and slippers. Her face was sad and tired, with lines where worry had dug furrows in her brow. Her hands were clasped as if in prayer. She looked to be in her late seventies and in excellent health. Her apartment was bare except for a single metal folding chair from a local funeral home. It sat in the middle of the living room. She took my hand and pulled me gently into the cold chair and sat me down before standing as tall as her tired bones could reach, and smiling.

As she stood before me, her hands came to life and her fingers reached for the sky. She briefly closed her eyes, filled with tears of joy, and opened them with a sparkle. As if in a dream, the light seemed to have dimmed. A warm sensation overwhelmed me, and my heart began to fill with anticipation. I couldn't remember feeling more content. I could feel my inner self begin to burst with excitement. My mind was a whirlwind of amazement and wonder. Nothing seemed more important than the sweet desire to be with the old black woman. I could feel for her and I wanted to be a part of her, whatever that was.

She smiled ever more softly, took a deep breath and began to sing. Her silver voice carried like golden bells from heaven as she sang her heart out like a champion Southern Baptist gospel singer. I remember vividly how shocked I felt to hear her sing with such clarity:

Amazing Grace, how sweet the sound . . .

My eyes began to tear with joy as I tried to choke back waves of pent-up frustration and emotion. Nothing seemed to matter anymore. I knew there was a reason for all of this, that there was something special about her.

. . . that saved a wretch like me.
I once was lost but now am found . . .

As I listened, the image of my long-dead sister materialized within my clouded mind. A feeling of complete helplessness and anger with God came together with the frustrations of my employment at Grady. The old black woman had shaken the cobwebs from the chambers of my tired heart and filled it with the mystery of the Lord.

> I was blind, but now I see.
> 'Twas grace that taught my heart to fear
> And grace my fears relieved.

As I listened intently to each word, I began to understand the purpose of my own being. This became the hour of my renewed faith in the Lord. It had been the worst week of my career in this business, and my regular partner, John, had already left on a much-needed vacation. Twice during this same week, I had considered suicide as a way out and off this planet. While I listened, I found myself taken back to a time when I straddled the railing of the hospital parking garage's fourth floor.

The stench of burned flesh and sticky sweet blood on my uniform continued to attack with a vengeance while forever reminding me of the horrified expression on the man's blackened and skin-splitting face. I couldn't stop vomiting long enough to catch my breath. I leaned a little further out and stared through my teary vision to the concrete sidewalk below. It would be so easy just to let gravity send me to my death.

Just an hour before, my temporary partner from day shift and I were eating a late dinner at McDonald's in East Point while watching the local fire department put out a fire in a garage apartment behind a house just across the street from us.

We realized that something was wrong with this picture when a private ambulance pulled up with lights flashing and siren blaring. I immediately called Fulton County 911. "Uh, 504 clear detail?" I was indicating that we were done with supper and hoping that we had not missed a call in our zone.

The dispatcher replied, "Received, 504. Return to your station."

My partner and I looked at each other, relieved. He was an FNG (fucking new guy) and couldn't afford to make a mistake since new EMTs were already a dime a dozen and could be easily replaced. I was in even greater peril. I anticipated that the hospital was just waiting for me to screw up so they could say, "I told you so!" My seniority with Grady EMS meant nothing. In the eyes of the administrators, I was equivalent to an FNG, even if I did have the lowest number as a basic EMT or ambulance driver.

We then wondered if the dispatcher even had us in service while a fire raged out of control across the street, three blocks from our station, and a private ambulance intruded on our call. "504 to Radio? You got a 33 in Zone 2 showing?" While I waited for a response, I noticed several firefighters dragging out a large bundle resembling a charred throw rug.

"Affirmative, 504. East Point workin' a 33 and a 67 on Main Street. Rescue en route at this time to assist private."

My partner asked by leaning into my ear, "Is she new?"

I stepped backward. "I ain't that deaf. Besides, I can't read your lips that close." He stepped backward and unconsciously began to pick his teeth.

The dispatcher apparently picked up on my concern about a fire in our zone and private sitting on top of our call. "Radio to 504, what's your 20?"

My partner took out a pen and searched for a piece of paper to write the call down on. "Forget it," I said. "This is going to be ours." I pointed across the street. Three EMTs had already reached the smoking bundle, and I realized then that it was a body that had been pulled out by the firefighters.

"Radio! 504 on top of 33. Rescue en route. East Point advised 10-8!"

My partner took off like a shot, and I grabbed him by the belt.

"Hey! We're Grady. Dammit, act like it." I said. I told him to get my bag and clipboard and I reminded him to walk, not run, to the smoking patient. "Okay, Radio, hold us out, and notify burn unit and 414 to get ramp clear."

The call turned into a fiasco straight from hell itself. A burn call from a fire is not something that can be handled with a set treatment. The textbook protocol learned in EMT school becomes a joke, and keeping the patient alive becomes a top priority. In this case hysteria ruled while the patient thrashed about in pain beyond agony. Hot, steaming blood spewed everywhere as we loaded him into our ambulance. Sterile water, all that could be found, splashed the cabinets, as we doused the man's body. Pieces of skin fell to the slippery floor and vomit dripped off the stretcher. A sheet of charred skin shed itself like a glove when I tried to hold his arm down for a quick IV stick. By the time we arrived at the hospital his stomach and chest had burst into four quadrants, and his face had become a hole where his mouth used to be. The world stopped when the back door opened.

Another EMT who was in the ER when we arrived told me later that he couldn't begin to describe what they found when they opened the back doors. He said that it was worse than anything he had ever seen in Vietnam. The ambulance was later taken out of service and towed away because no one wanted to get in it and drive it off the ramp. Everything in it—papers, medical supplies, and the like—was shoveled out and taken away to be burned. The patient, a man in his early thirties, had just learned that he had tested positive for the HIV virus. He had returned home, soaked himself with lighter fluid, and struck a match.

Again, I thought how gravity would be so easy. I could just tip myself over a bit and let nature do the rest. A firm hand rested on my shoulder just as I was about to let myself go. I looked back and was surprised, even embarrassed, to see a bearded blue-eyed man in a Grady EMS uniform standing between two parked cars. He was carrying a metal clipboard with a worn Bible. He smiled and turned to a page in the Bible, and while he scanned the page with a long finger, I read softly to myself the verse that seemed to be highlighted in the dark of the night:

Praise the Lord, O my soul. I will praise the Lord all my life.
I will sing praises to my God as long as I live.

I began to smile deep within my heart. My irrational thoughts turned back to reality as I felt a thirst to find the true meaning of the verse. The man somehow sensed my eagerness and turned to another verse. My heart began to slow down and my mind began to focus.

The Lord upholds all those who fall and lifts up all who are bowed down.

I could feel a giant weight being lifted off my shoulders. I smiled back at him and asked for more reassurance. I needed more answers. Just then, I heard a siren wailing from behind the hospital, and I watched it turn the corner for the concrete ramp and the emergency room. When I turned back, the man was gone. I ran to the other side of the parking garage and looked for him down the exit stairway, only to find nothing. I spent the next week looking for him by describing him to my fellow workers and going through the roster of other EMTs, to no avail. I decided to put it in the back of my mind. At least I got a good night's sleep for the first time in months. It was not booze and pot that induced this sleep, but the comfort of the words from the Bible that protected me from the evil of nightmares.

> This grace has brought me safe thus far,
> And grace will lead me home.

The old black woman sang the last verse with a final burst of energy that radiated with the love of God. The Lord was reaching out to us! We could feel his almighty and spiritual presence. Her face lit up and her eyes looked with hunger toward the heaven that she knew she was promised. She knew that there'd be no more sorrow, no unhappiness nor trouble, for she saw that there would be peace in the valley for her someday. She raised her hands, palms outward, and bowed her gray head as if she were listening to the Lord talking to her. She gently shook her head and occasionally nodded in agreement.

She bent down to take my hands into hers. Her youthful eyes looked into mine and I could see clearly into forever. She smiled again to reassure me that she had found what she was looking for, and I smiled back to show her how happy I was so for her. And then, she died.

8

The Fat Lady

*I*t took more than fifty months on the streets to be able to count myself among the 20 EMTs with the most seniority of the 140 employed in the department. The fact that I was finally able to command respect from others despite my disability was the highlight of my career. It was also around this time that I began to feel "burned out."

Some weeks later, I found myself in her office. She sat in her chair, with long legs crossed and hands folded while her elbows rested on her knees. Behind her, on the wall, several diplomas hung in a neat row, testifying to her credentials with the Clayton County Mental Health Service. She had already taken the phone off the hook and locked the door to ensure privacy. After a few moments, she asked, "Did she visit you?" I heard her, but I couldn't comprehend what she was asking me. From the tone of her voice, I could surmise that it was a question. I have extreme difficulty hearing females because of my high-frequency hearing loss.

I got up and turned the chair around to face her. "Sorry," I said. "I don't hear too well and I need to read your lips."

She straightened up in her chair and recrossed her legs. "Oh, I'm sorry! Sure, that's fine. How is it now?" she asked with embarrassment.

"Fine now. Just talk normally and we'll be fine."

"Sure. Okay . . . we talked last week about your nightmare. Has she visited you since then?"

"No, she hasn't."

She waited a few more moments. "Are you still drinking to sleep?"

I thought about that one for a minute. If not this problem, then something else.

"Yes," I finally said.

She jotted down a note on her pad. "Are you ready to talk about it today?"

I shuddered and took a couple of deep breaths to help shake off the chill. "Yes," I answered.

"Go on." She leaned forward.

"Will this get back to Grady somehow? I'm afraid that I could get into some serious trouble."

She leaned back in her chair and laughed. "Of course not! Not unless you killed somebody."

I said nothing and looked off toward the window. She leaned forward again when she realized that I was serious. "I don't know," I said. "She said I did."

"Who said you did?"

"The fat lady keeps tellin' me that I killed her."

"Is she the one from your nightmare?" she asked with concern.

"Yeah. She keeps comin' every now and then."

"Why don't you tell me what happened."

I remember it was damn hot, and I was working a double shift for a friend. The weatherman said it was already 105 degrees, with no relief in sight. I had a new partner who was on her very first day on the job. She had just come out of three months of training and orientation before the department assigned her to me. I appreciated that, because it showed they trusted me to break in new people.

Anyway, as soon as we went into service, the dispatcher handed us a call for a woman not breathing. The call was only half a block away, so we got there in less than a minute. Standing outside this apartment building was a bunch of people carrying on and crying while pointing upstairs. I assumed that it was a natural law of some sort that sick people were required to live on the third floor or higher while the healthy ones lived on the first floor. We went upstairs and into this dark apartment. It stank to high heaven as we followed a foot trail among the garbage strewn everywhere. We arrived at the kitchen, and the smell was even worse there. I was sure an animal had died in there, but this little girl kept pulling on my shirt and saying that her mother wasn't breathing.

The little girl pointed to the far corner of the kitchen, where I saw something that resembled a beached whale. I walked gingerly over to it, bent down, and saw that a large breast was covering her face. I moved it to one side. Her face was just a slab of meat with two beady eyes. She wasn't breathing and her skin was incredibly dry and tight to the touch. My partner was anxious to prove herself, and she got down and tried to find a pulse. I had told her that it was impossible. The veins were buried deep in the fat. It was impossible to check the carotid artery—she had no neck. I tried to find a pulse somewhere else, and finally found one in the crook of her arm. I couldn't believe it.

What was I going to do with 900 pounds of dead weight in full arrest? Before I tried to become a hero, I needed to consider what was involved. In a matter of seconds, I considered all the options, including the manpower required just to get her ready for transport. Some construction and renovation would be inevitable, involving the removal of the door, the door frame, and at least two feet of bricks, just to get her out of the kitchen. Did we need a crane, or could we drag her through the hole and down three flights of rusting metal steps? We would need utility ropes. Keep in mind that CPR must be maintained throughout the call once the decision has been made to provide life support. We would also have to call for a pickup truck, because I knew she would never fit in the back of the ambulance.

I looked my partner in the eye and told her to go back to the truck and wait for me. She knew that I had found a weak pulse. She already had her portable radio out and was ready to call for assistance. I told her no. I was serious, and she knew it. Other people had told her that it would be wise to listen to me if I thought something was wrong. She didn't say another word, and left quietly for the truck to wait for me.

Meanwhile, the fat lady just kept hanging on. Her pulse was weak and getting weaker, slowing down from eighteen to eight per minute. I still couldn't see what I could possibly do for her. I tried to think of any options that I might have missed. I was fearful that the administrators would get wind of this and have me fired. I was still debating whether I should call this in via landline to cover my ass or keep quiet about it and claim she was already dead when I arrived. I made up my mind that there wasn't anything that anybody could do for her. As far as I was concerned, she had signed her own death certificate.

The whole family came into the kitchen after my partner left, still crying and carrying on. They kept asking me if she was going to be all right. I just reached down and pulled up the sheet to cover her up, told them that she had passed on and gone home to the Lord. Oooooh, man! They all started falling down like flies, crying and screaming at the Lord.

I was doing a little hard praying myself: Oh Jesus! I'm so sorry. I didn't know what to do. I had to let her go on and die. She just kept hanging on. There wasn't anything I could do. Oh, Lord!

I had had enough. I felt lower than the scales on the belly of a slithering snake for playing the role of God and making a decision I would have to be responsible for, and maybe even pay for, sooner or later. I had lied when I said she was dead. In fact, she was still barely alive. She just needed a little assistance and I wouldn't give it to her. My last sin was to pray that she was dead before I walked out. When I got back to the truck, my partner gave me the silent treatment. She asked me if I had found a pulse, and I simply said no. She couldn't argue with me. She hadn't found one either, and I had seniority.

My partner was doing the usual paperwork, and we were waiting for APD to come and sign off before the funeral people got there. I was watching the apartment on the third floor, and I kept imagining the family members running back outside and telling us she was still alive. I was terrified at the prospect. I was also counting on APD to take their time. I wanted to make sure that the fat lady was dead before she was taken away. That made me feel even lower. Surely I was going to burn in hell for this.

We waited a while longer as more people gathered around the apartment building. I was beginning to get paranoid. They started to point toward us as if I were being accused of something. Ten minutes later a white Cadillac with huge tailfins pulled up in front of us. A big fat black man, dressed in white and chomping on a cigar, got out and walked over to my side of the truck. He asked me where the deceased was, and I simply pointed through the windshield toward the people on the third floor. I told him that I thought he was going to have to get another funeral home to come help him on this one. He looked at me as if I had insulted him. He kept on walking and got real friendly with the family before disappearing inside. A few minutes later he came out and got back in his car to drive away. I thought he was going for the cops or to call somebody down at the State Medical Board to have my number revoked and me put on death row. Still, the cops hadn't shown up yet, and I was debating whether to go back inside and check again for a pulse, when a tow truck arrived with people on it. It had a flat bed in the back, with a winch.

I was beginning to feel queasy. They all went upstairs with ropes, hammers, and sheets. I was curious and decided to risk going back in. What I saw was beyond belief. Several workers were knocking chunks of bricks from around the metal door frame, removing enough to make a hole big enough to pull the fat lady through. While they were doing that, the others tied ropes around her in preparation for removing her from the mattress she had lived on for the past twenty years. A family member had to quickly take possession of the fat lady's TV, makeup kit, some rotting food, and alarm clock.

The next problem was how to get her down to the ground floor without rolling her off the balcony. The stairway was only three or four feet wide and constructed of cheap metal railing. They bent the railing over as far as it would go and tugged on the fat lady until they reached the first landing. They pushed, pulled, and shoved her between the railing and the brick wall. Now for the easy part. They simply let gravity do its job with a firm jerk on the rope.

She slid down like hot butter running off a plate while her head bumped and cracked on each step.

I felt so damn guilty. I kept trying to tell myself that it was all her damn fault. She just had to pick this day, on my shift, at a time when I just happened to be half a block away. Shit!

Now the fat lady was on the ground floor, and they backed the truck up between the buildings. The driver got out, climbed onto the back and yanked out a hitch connected to a wire cable. It all seemed so unreal and so slow. I remember how hard it was to walk in my combat boots. They just kept sticking to the pavement.

I felt a reassuring hand on my shoulder. "Do you think she will be back to visit you?" the counselor asked.

"Yeah. Pretty sure she will. She'll take her time."

"There was nothing you could have done for her. If I had been in the same situation, I honestly don't know what I would have done. It takes a very brave and special person to be an EMT."

"No," I said. "It takes a damn fool! No matter. What bothers me is that I could have made an effort to revive her and get her out, but I didn't." I thought about what I had just said, and I changed my mind. "No, I'm not sorry for what I did. I'll deal with it somehow." I got up to go. I tried to tell her that it takes one to know one, to understand the hell I am trying to talk about. But to hell with it, . . . better the fat lady than me.

9

The Deaf Patient

*I*n 1964 an acoustic coupler was invented and modified
for the telephone by a deaf scientist, Dr. Robert Wie-
brecht. This device allowed deaf people to communicate
with each other over telephone lines.

In the more than thirty years of steady progress in the
development of the telecommunications device for the deaf
(TDD), coupled with passage of the Americans with Disabilities Act, federal, state, and local telecommunication services for the speech and hearing impaired have expanded.
The issue of deaf accessibility to emergency response
through 911 is still controversial, however.

Much of the criticism directed to a specific 911 communication center, as described in the publication *Silent News,*
has been unjustified. Careful investigation of some of the
complaints reveals valid reasons for the failure of a 911 center to respond. Incoming deaf emergency calls are still rare
and are usually not responded to as promptly as calls involving voice communication. The installation of the TDD
would be a vast improvement over no communication at
all, and the device also constitutes full compliance with the
federal law.

There are more than 24 million people in the United
States who suffer from some type of hearing impairment.

Of that number, there are 350,000 to 2 million who are profoundly deaf. The hearing-impaired population is expected to increase in the coming years, due to noise pollution, disease, injury, and old age. The availability of TDDs when requesting emergency response will inevitably grow along with a growing deaf population. Someday the device may be as common as the pocket calculator in most American households. Public safety officials have both a moral and a legal obligation to respond to the needs of deaf and disabled people.

A situation that was in the news a few years ago will illustrate the problems faced by deaf patients in medical situations. In a remote corner of a small poverty-stricken county, an hour south of the city of Atlanta, volunteer EMTs and firefighters responded from their homes and jobs to a cardiac call at the home of a deaf family. After the usual delay in picking up the ambulance, the first responders arrived to find complete chaos.

An elderly deaf man was complaining of severe chest pain and had collapsed on the kitchen floor. Communication with the patient was not an option. The call became an immediate "load and go." The man was immediately transported and stabilized with a line of saline solution and full oxygen to the nearest emergency room, at a small county general hospital that could best be compared to a glorified clinic in an industrial plant. The EMT assumed that the family would meet them at the hospital and be able to give details about the man's medical history and allergies. Instead, the family arrived at Clayton County General Hospital to find that the man hadn't been taken there.

Upon arrival at the ER, the man was handed off to a charge nurse. At this time, the man began to point frantically at his chest, indicating pain. The nurse spoke to the man, asking if he was allergic to any medication. He responded by shaking his head from side to side in concert with his ever-increasing pain. Naturally, the nurse took this to mean that he had no allergies to medication. The nurse had not been told by the EMT that the man was deaf. She rechecked his IV line and then left to prepare his medication according to the standard treatment protocols for a cardiac patient. A phone call was placed to the physician on call for the hospital, for permission to administer the medication, but his whereabouts were unknown. Shortly thereafter, an injection of morphine was given, which induced massive cardiac arrest, and the patient died. None of the medical personnel knew that the man was allergic to morphine.

Information about the initial contact to 911 was not confirmed, pending an investigation. A spokesperson for the county commission involved refused to speculate on the case. The county did have a 911 center, but not an enhanced system. A system enhancer would have given the dispatcher the advantage of a call-back number and an address of the caller through the computer system. A source at EMS headquarters confirmed that a TDD was in service during the time in question. When the deaf call came in, the dispatcher answered and allegedly did not get a response, other than a GA (short for Go Ahead). The dispatcher did not know what this meant, so he hung up, thinking it was a prank call. A second call from a hearing neighbor confirmed that the man was having a heart attack.

Most EMTs have no prior experience with deaf patients. If a deaf patient is found unconscious, the attending EMT would probably never know of the disability unless informed directly by a family member or neighbor, or unless a hearing aid is visible. The EMT would understandably begin treatment as if the person is a normal hearing patient, without consideration for his disability. If the deaf patient is conscious and his condition does not present an immediate medical emergency, the EMT would attempt voice communication, assuming that the patient could read lips. The possibility of using a pad and pencil is often overlooked. Gleaning information verbally from a deaf patient is extremely difficult, and sometimes the patient inadvertently conveys the opposite of what he intends. American Sign Language, when rendered in writing, is usually confusing to a hearing person.

According to information provided by a local deaf organization in Atlanta, there is a deaf population of just under 70,000 living and working in the metropolitan area. When I asked for the source of the information, I was told that the figures were based primarily on an "educated" guess. The information was certainly not derived from a United States census report. As an EMT I encountered deaf people from poor and underprivileged backgrounds. I came to think of them as the "Uninformed." From my frustrating attempts at conversing with them in sign language, I could only conclude that most had had little or no education. They spoke their own dialects, along with American Sign Language used in a "street smart" way. Most of these people are unaware of the Americans with Disabilities Act and the benefits that could accrue from it. Deaf organizations and social service groups have failed to reach out to these people. They seem to feel that these people must come to them first.

Many of the parents of these kids have interpreted their child's deafness as a punishment from God. Discrimination against these people is the norm. My observation of a typical

"Uninformed" person is that the average life expectancy is eighteen years. There is likely to be excessive substance abuse—glue sniffing, paint sniffing, crack, or alcohol—as well as malnutrition, improper hygiene, and a lack of adequate medical care. It was not unusual for me to hear from time to time that a dead man encountered on an emergency call was a "mute."

Most EMTs who have never had prior experience with a deaf patient will more than likely meet up with the "Uninformed" at some time during their career. It only takes one bad apple to spoil the rest of the barrel. That one bad apple can instill in an EMT's mind a permanent impression of "Deaf and Dumb" that will affect any subsequent encounter with a deaf person.

After my service with Grady EMS I determined that I would somehow plug the gap between the "Uninformed" and public safety services. I established Tri-Communication Emergency Medical Service for the Deaf in Atlanta. Tri-Comm EMS provided a private ambulance service for the hard of hearing and deaf people who requested it. The service was fully equipped to respond to all medical emergencies and trauma situations, including transportation to hospitals. It had mobile telephones and TDDs, both in the dispatcher's office and the truck, for immediate communication with the patients at their homes. My employees were learning sign language in on-the-job training while responding to deaf calls. Tri-Comm also provided an Outreach Medical Program for deaf patients who requested it. After a year I was forced to close the business, either because people didn't want to use it or because they didn't understand how to use it.

I found that providing a private ambulance service for

the deaf is practically impossible, even in a market where there were more than 70,000 deaf people. Thousands of dollars went into advertising, and I was invited to speak and explain my service to many clubs and organizations throughout the metropolitan Atlanta area. The support that I received convinced me that the service was needed. The problem arose from the fact that I had failed to research the "payment received" aspect of the business. The other private ambulance services were able to take a wide variety of patients who possessed private insurance, Medicare, or state Medicaid insurance, while Tri-Comm EMS was forced to accept mostly Medicaid patients, predominantly deaf Social Security recipients. It was rare to find one with private insurance.

The state of Georgia provides Medicaid for those who are unable to get regular medical insurance. Among the problems that this presents is that a Medicaid recipient is forced to search for a physician who is willing to accept a Medicaid patient. The state would pay only a certain amount of money for my private service. If the call was an emergency, and if it was dispatched by Fulton County 911, my service could collect from both Medicaid and the county. The state would not pay for any treatment that might be necessary during transport to the hospital. This applied not only to deaf people, but also to the general population. A person with a private insurance carrier, however, can expect the royal treatment.

Of those deaf patients that did have private insurance, many didn't want to use their insurance for fear of raising premium costs. The cost they were worried about was actually the deductible that had to be paid in order to use the insurance. The Medicaid recipients believed that they would receive a bill from the state if they used the service, while others simply gave up trying to find a physician who would accept a Medicaid patient. Instead, they would spend days waiting in line at Grady Hospital for treatment.

The reality was that only one out of nine deaf patients used Tri-Comm EMS for emergency response, and most of them still owe Tri-Comm. The others called to ask us to interpret in the emergency room. When we asked why they hadn't called us for the emergency in the first place, they would say, "I didn't want to bother you." After receiving several of these requests, a local hearing interpreter organization contacted me and asked me to stop providing interpreting services for deaf patients at hospitals. According to them, we were not qualified, and I didn't want to spend almost $900 to become "qualified" through their program. They then asked that Tri-Comm contact them whenever an emergency call came in from a deaf patient so that they could provide interpreting between the doctors and nurses and the patient.

"Could you be more specific?" I asked.

"Call us before you go on the call," I was told.

That was all I needed to hear. "Look," I said, "first of all, I don't give a damn, and no, I will not cooperate with you. It is up to the patient to decide who to call for interpreting services."

The woman on the other end of the phone interrupted. "No, the hospital is required by law to contact us, and so are you."

"Wait! You're talking about a hospital that is funded in part by federal monies that are required to meet certain guidelines . . . ," but it was pointless to argue with them.

It was not long before I was forced to ask Fulton County for a spot on their rotation list, just to keep the business afloat until I could resolve this situation with the interpreters.

The 911 dispatchers often wonder why deaf people don't use the system as often as they might. It was rare to get a deaf emergency call through the TDD at the 911 office. I used to spend time at the 911 center when we were between calls, if we were assigned to the zone that included the center. I would always ask if any calls had come through the TDD, and I would invariably get a negative response. It had gotten to the point where the TDD was pushed back away from the main radio console and forgotten. Once in a while, I'd drag it up front, blow the dust off it, and call a deaf friend, just to see if it still worked. Then I'd have the friend call me back through the 911 system and watch the dispatcher pick it up. She answered, "911, Fulton County. What is your emergency?" The same dispatcher would repeat the question, then hang up the phone and go back to working the police band. I walked over and asked if she had heard some signal tones of the phone, and she replied, "Yes, I did, now that you mention it. Doesn't that mean a deaf caller or something?"

During the course of my career I became convinced that there are three different classes of deaf people. In the first category are the deaf people who receive a true deaf education. In the second are those who were mainstreamed into the public school system, and in the third category are those who have been neglected since birth, the most unfortunate. The aforementioned "Uninformed" are often considered to be mentally retarded by their own parents. They receive little or no education and are severely poverty stricken. A good number of them do not receive help from either Social Security or Medicaid. Most of them were born at Grady and will continue to patronize the hospital for years to come.

Grady Hospital is funded almost entirely by tax dollars from Fulton and DeKalb counties, and free medical services are provided to anyone who needs them.

When employed by Cherokee County EMS, after leaving Grady and before I started Tri-Comm EMS for the Deaf, I discovered a unique population of deaf people— mountain folks from the remote areas of the north Georgia mountains. In many cases these people had grown up with no knowledge of sign language. Their parents had improvised by inventing hand signals. One family had lived in the same house for generations without the comfort of central heat, hot water, or a bathroom. The most education that anyone, deaf or hearing, obtained would be the sixth grade. One eighteen-year-old girl that I met was the fourteenth child of parents who were in their sixties. She had never attended school. Her parents thought she was a punishment from God.

Being a patient in a prehospital setting will continue to be problematic for deaf people. I don't see an easy solution to the dilemma and can't offer any suggestions for improvement. Any recommendations would have to embrace people from all geographic areas, as well as all financial and educational levels, in order to come up with a set of rules that would apply to all 911 centers, law enforcement agencies, fire departments, and other emergency service personnel. This is basically unrealistic.

Classifications of deafness cannot be limited to simple audiological variations, but should also include the different types of people who are deaf. Each deaf patient presents a unique challenge, even for me.

Afterword

My intention in writing this book was twofold: first, to make people aware of the problems faced by deaf patients in prehospital settings, and second, to illustrate the numerous limitations and obstacles that I faced daily in my quest to serve as a deaf firefighter and EMT.

Somehow I survived the streets, Grady EMS, and the horseplay of my fellow firefighters at various fire stations. To this day I don't know how. It took a lot out of me; made me dead tired in both mind and body. After a decade and a half, I hung up my bulletproof vest and put away the tiny .25-caliber automatic. I wanted to leave it all before it killed me. I rode with many partners, but only one remained faithful, always on time, and willing to work overtime. I cheated him as many times as he snatched innocent and deserving lives from me. He has been called many names since the beginning of civilization, but I knew him simply as the Grim Reaper.

If I had it to do over again, I wouldn't. For years I have envied people who had nine-to-five jobs and came home to a secure family. As it is, I suffer from frequent headaches, memory loss, nervousness, loss of balance, and severe tinnitus. I look forward to the day when I can forget it ever happened.

The question remains—Is it really possible for a deaf person to become a firefighter or an emergency medical technician? I have proven that it is possible, but aspects of the question can still be researched, analyzed, and argued. I have concluded that being a firefighter or an EMT requires some residual hearing and the ability to communicate verbally. After all, we must consider the safety of the patient, as well as of the partner.

A young woman who aspired to be a rescue worker for a local EMS outfit in her county came to me for advice. We had several conversations in which I encouraged her to pursue her dream, but I felt responsible for laying out some serious scenarios that could impede her goal. She had some residual hearing and her speech was passable, but she told me that she would be unable to communicate on a radio, even though she could hear talking in the background. I told her that that would be her first obstacle. She insisted that she could depend on help from her partner. I explained to her that teamwork on an EMS crew meant that each member of that crew has a specific set of responsibilities on any given call. One person can't do the job of two and at the same time provide quality care for patients. It might mean the difference between life and death for both patient and crew. The driver can't do the technician's job, and vice versa.

Among the problems for a deaf EMT is the difficulty of communicating on the radio while driving. If the technician is doing CPR, the driver might have to relay information to the hospital at the same time. If the technician is deaf and the patient is having respiratory difficulty, the driver can't pull over to the side of the road and assist the technician in determining breath sounds to initiate the proper treatment. The same young woman interjected that there would be others on board to help her. I asked her, "All the time? Highly unlikely." There are always times when you find yourself alone with someone's life in the balance.

I was able to take advantage of modern technology when my mother discovered a device that gave me a visual read-out for heart, pulse, breathing rates, and even blood pressure. It wasn't long before the device became popular even with the hearing EMTs. That was the only piece of equipment, other than my hearing aid, that helped me do my job without specifically using what was left of my profound hearing loss.

I often had some difficulty in hearing breath sounds such as rales, wheezing, and congestion while en route to a hospital with the siren going. An ambulance is not exactly soundproof when the siren box is on. It was not uncommon for EMTs to suffer some degree of hearing loss. One of the definitions listed under deafness in the dictionary implies that siren deafness is considered a form of hearing loss. During my stint as maintenance coordinator for the ambulance department we recommended that the siren be re-mounted to the front bumper of the truck to keep the siren out and away from the crew.

If that failed, I could always resort to turning off my hearing aid and using it as an earplug. By turning it off and leaving the stethoscope in my ears I could concentrate on what I was hearing from the patient. This is similar to what a hearing person does by putting a finger in one ear while trying to hear with the other. Unfortunately, no one has invented a device that would provide a deaf EMT with a digital read-out of the many types of breath sounds that could help determine the nature of a shortness-of-breath complaint. Such a device would give the deaf EMT the edge that is needed to help another deaf EMT perform on a par with his co-workers.

Communicating on the radio was a daily struggle, but it was not as bad as I was afraid it would be. At Grady EMS, almost all the radio traffic broadcast over the EMS tactical channel consisted of codes and signals with numbers. This worked to my advantage, since I was more proficient in communicating with signals and codes than in regular conversation. As long as we stuck to codes and signals, most people never realized that I was deaf.

Talking to a doctor on the hospital frequency was mainly a matter of following a simple format that I borrowed from the trip report. My partner would listen for any response that I might have missed, just in case. If I couldn't understand the doctor, or if I had my hands full, my partner would simply pick up the microphone mounted on the dashboard and take over the radio.

Dr. I. King Jordan, the deaf president of Gallaudet University, was quoted as saying, "A deaf person can do anything." I was watching him on television, in the vending machine area of the Ely Center on the campus of the same university. I had returned after almost seventeen years to see a tremendous change in all aspects of deaf culture, including the remarkable transformation of the Gallaudet campus. It was almost lockup time at the university, and I stood amid empty tables and chairs. The interviewer asked Jordan, "What could a deaf person do?"

The president replied with a confident smile on his face, ". . . a banker, possibly a firefighter, . . ." I couldn't help but smile. I wondered if he knew just how possible it really was to be a deaf firefighter.

Just recently I learned that a deaf woman in Erie, Pennsylvania, is working as an EMT for a local private ambulance service. I have heard from a young man in a western state who is a member of a local volunteer fire department, but he complains bitterly about the imposed restrictions. He is still not allowed inside a fire call or to perform fire suppressions and is usually assigned to water supply or cleaning the station. In Leesburg, Virginia, a young man who is not deaf but is confined to a wheelchair is a volunteer member of a fire station. Although his MS prevents him from responding on calls, he has become a valuable member by maintaining the station through administrative duties. These reports are indeed encouraging, but we still have a long way to go.

I have read letters from those who aspire to be an EMT or a firefighter and have talked to many who desire to know how to start. How to get started is the most common question asked. Do I have to hear to be one is the second most common question asked. I personally believe that it does not matter how much one can hear. A deaf person can do anything, and it is our responsibility to make a better world for our next deaf generation.

We're getting there, slowly but surely. I hope that I have done my part.

Abbreviations Used in This Book

ADA — Americans with Disabilities Act

ASL — American Sign Language

APD — Atlanta Police Department

CPR — cardiopulmonary resuscitation

DOA — dead on arrival

EMS — emergency medical service

EMT — emergency medical technician

EOA — esophageal obturator airway

ER — emergency room

ETA — estimated time of arrival

SOP — standard operating procedure

TDD — telecommunications device for the deaf

Codes and Signals

Code 1 — Nonemergency response

Code 2 — Use lights and extreme caution when responding

Code 3 — Lights and siren used, emergency response

Code 4 — Situation under control

10–1 — Repeat traffic

10–4 — Message received

10–8 — In service

10–24 — Demented person

10–32 — Return to hospital or station

10–33 — Fire call

10–50 — Gunshot

10–51 — Knife

10–95 — Mechanical problems

About the Author

S teven Schrader lives in North Georgia with his wife, Nancy Carol, and their dog, Vada. He is currently writing a novel and a historical account of the activities of deaf Civil War soldiers.

He began his writing career as a compiler of the Battle of Jonesborough special section that appeared in the October 1981 *Clayton News-Daily*. Many of his editorial comments regarding the Americans with Disabilities Act and the 911 system have also been published.